Living
Fully

Dying
Well

Living Fully Dying Well

Reflecting on Death to Find Your Life's Meaning

Edward W. Bastian, Ph.D., and Tina L. Staley, L.C.S.W.

with Rabbi Zalman Schachter-Shalomi · Tessa Bielecki
Dr. Ira Byock · Mirabai Starr
Dr. Marilyn M. Schlitz · Joan Halifax Roshi
Edited by Netanel Miles-Yepez

Sounds True, Inc.
Boulder, CO 80306

© 2009 Edward W. Bastian and Tina L. Staley

SOUNDS TRUE is a trademark of Sounds True, Inc.

All rights reserved. Published 2009.
Printed in Canada

Book design by Karen Polaski

ISBN 978-1-59179-701-2

10 9 8 7 6 5 4 3 2 1

Library of Congress Cataloging-in-Publication Data
Bastian, Edward W.
        Living fully, dying well : reflecting on death to find your life's meaning /
Edward W. Bastian and Tina L. Staley; with Zalman Schachter-Shalomi ... [et al.] ;
edited by Netanel Miles-Yepez.
        p. cm.
        Includes bibliographical references (p. 267) and index.
        ISBN 978-1-59179-701-2
        1. Death—Religious aspects. 2. Spiritual life. 3. Death—Religious
aspects—Meditations. 4. Spiritual exercises. I. Staley, Tina L. II. Miles-Yepez,
Netanel. III. Title.
        BL504.B37 2009
        202'.3—dc22
                                                2008054816

Death has many profound meanings, providing keys for unlocking the infinite potential of our being. The book is dedicated to those who have the simple courage to explore these meanings, to embrace their consequences, to die in wondrous ways, and to experience the marvelous fullness of life.

EDWARD W. BASTIAN

For Jeannie Renchard, Tom Klutznick, and my mom and dad, Janey and Gabriel Stahle, whose passion and participation in life have made me live more fully.

TINA L. STALEY

And to die is different from what anyone supposed, and luckier.

WALT WHITMAN
Leaves of Grass

Contents

Note to the Reader

This book is comprised of two distinct parts. The first is a dialogue between a number of leading spiritual teachers, scientists, and social workers concerning the spiritual, medical, scientific, and psychological aspects of dying, as well as their perspectives on the afterlife. The second part is an independent collection of resources: guided meditations, life-review practices, affirmations, and reflections. While Part I is intended to be read sequentially in order to answer questions and give new perspectives, Part II can be used according to your own interest or need; no particular order need be followed. However, for those of you who are inspired to use Parts I and II in a more integrated fashion—doing the exercises in coordination with the text—various parallel exercises from Part II are referenced in the text where similar exercises are mentioned.   —*Ed.*

Introduction

Not so long ago, I found myself propped up in bed, gazing at the light flooding through my window and feeling tremendously grateful for one more day of life. In that pristine stillness of dawn, as the dark of night was transformed into the light of day—*I was reborn*. After a second brush with death, I felt I had genuinely awakened to something new, to a kind of love and gratitude that at sixty years old I had never known before.

Over the last several years, death has become so present for me—not in a morbid or fearful way, but as an inescapable reality to understand, to prepare for, and hopefully to move through with wisdom, compassion, and purpose. For me, there was no avoiding it; over a relatively short span of time I had lost my father, Kenneth, my beloved "little" brother, Kenny, my dear cousin Bruce, several uncles, and many close friends, and—twice—I had nearly lost my own life. The first time, I was thought to be dead from the sting of a single bee.

THE WAKE-UP CALL

It happened on a snowy winter night in 1997. I walked through the door of my home in Woody Creek, near Aspen, Colorado, with my friend George Stranahan after a neighborhood meeting to chat a bit before he headed home. We strolled into the living room, shed our winter boots, and I slipped on a pair of warm slippers. Immediately, I felt a painful sting on the bottom of my right foot. The sting was a shock, but I wasn't worried since I had never been allergic to bee stings before. I kicked off the slipper and out dropped the bee, which I gently deposited in the snow outside my door for his last moments of life. George began to kid me about not being "a good Buddhist," sending the poor bee out to a certain death in the freezing snow. I reminded him that the bee was about to die anyway, having lost his stinger, and that the cold would numb him into sleep, and he would die peacefully. George, of course, didn't buy this and continued to kid me.

I turned on the cold water in the kitchen sink and stuck my foot under the water to bring down the swelling. Then, pulling a couple of beers out of the refrigerator, George and I were just about to sit down for a chat when I suddenly felt dizzy. "George," I said, "something is happening . . ." Alarmed at my expression, he led me to a seat where I collapsed and began to lose consciousness. The last thing I heard was George calling 911.

The next thing I remember was being spread out on my back on the living room floor fighting to breathe. Looking up over the edges of an oxygen mask, I saw the cigarette-toting face of my next-door neighbor, Hunter S. Thompson, the famed "Gonzo journalist," yelling at me, "Live, damn it, live!" Other neighbors, Jillian and Oliver, were also standing around me with deep concern on their faces. Hunter had been called by my good friend, Sheriff Bob Braudis, who heard the 911 ambulance call from his walkie-talkie at home. When Hunter received the call, he and our buddy Oliver had rushed up to my house.

The paramedics lifted me onto a stretcher and hauled me off to the hospital. Lying there on my hospital bed, it began to dawn on me what had just happened. After all my years of study of Buddhism and spiritual practice, in both India and the United States, I had simply lost consciousness and was utterly vulnerable to whatever happened next. As soon as I was able to sit up on the bed, I told my friend Bob how humbled—even a little humiliated—I was by having "died" so unconsciously, without any spiritual prayers or meditation. It was a hell of a wake-up call.

A BUDDHIST SOJOURN

You have to understand where I was coming from; back in the 1970s, I was studying, writing, and making a film in India as a Fulbright Fellow. My goals were to complete my Ph.D. research on the Buddhist scriptures called "The Perfection of Wisdom Sutras," to write the results of my research, and to complete a film about a famous Tibetan Buddhist refugee monastery called Sera, where I lived for a year of my two-year stint in India. During the other year, I studied with great Tibetan *geshes* and Indian *panditas* in Dharamsala, Sarnath, Varanasi, and Bodh Gaya.

Varanasi is the spiritual center of India, where thousands of people come to die and to be cremated on the banks of the Ganges River, where their ashes are strewn and corpses float along the shores. In Varanasi, death is looked at straight in the face every day. There is little fear because there is unquestioned faith in the reincarnation of the immortal soul. Living there was a seminal experience in my life. I learned to see life from a perspective that was quite different from our American one, where no one talks about or prepares for death, where so many seem to think that they will be the one exception when it comes to death.

During that period, I also traveled to Bodh Gaya with my teacher, Geshe Sopa, and several friends to attend teachings by the Dalai Lama. Bodh Gaya is a very poor town, yet it is a magnet for Buddhists throughout the world, who all come to prostrate, meditate, and pray there. The center of attraction is an enormous *stupa* (shrine) commemorating the Buddha. Just outside the stupa is the famed Bodhi tree under which the Buddha achieved enlightenment. Actually, it is said that this tree came from a cutting from a tree in Sri Lanka that grew from a cutting of the original tree in Bodh Gaya.

One afternoon in Bodh Gaya, I was introduced to Geshe Donyo, a middle-aged Tibetan lama who had been the student of my teacher, Geshe Sopa, in Tibet before they fled the Chinese invasion. Because of our relationship with the same esteemed teacher, we quickly became good friends, and he became my teacher as well because of his far superior knowledge, deep practice, and seniority. Later that year, I visited and studied with him at the Tantric monastery called Gyudmed in southern India. A wise, jocular, and patient teacher, who, like many other Tibetans is just plain fun to be around, Geshe Donyo became the abbot of Sera Monastery, home to nearly five thousand monks. He is present in each moment, always ready to help, constantly compassionate, wise, and lighthearted. But whenever we parted and I'd say something in Tibetan that was typically American, like, "See you later," he invariably replied with a big smile: "If I don't die." Ever since we first met, I have known that Geshe-la's jovial, wise, and compassionate attitude is intrinsically linked to his own attitude and preparedness for death.[1]

At Bodh Gaya, my Tibetan teachers and I sat on the ground for several days listening to the teachings of the Dalai Lama. During his introductory talk, His Holiness emphasized the impermanence of our being, the interdependence of all that exists, the relationship between compassion and our own eternal happiness, and the potential for each and every one of us to become an enlightened, compassionate Buddha.

Since that time, I have become both experientially and intellectually convinced that each of us has a subtle core consciousness that is always in a state of change, and that this consciousness has the potential for ultimate happiness, wisdom, and compassion. It is the ever-changing core consciousness that incarnates itself as a new body, life after life, until it is liberated from the causes of suffering and rebirth. This potential for liberation and enlightenment was demonstrated by the Buddha and the founders of all the world's great spiritual traditions. They have shown us that our consciousness contains (depending on our spiritual tradition) Buddha Nature, the Holy Spirit, Divine Indwelling, Divine Love, or Christ Consciousness. And this divine potential of our core consciousness can expand to pervade our entire being if we will only engage wholeheartedly in spiritual practice.

Since my predominate training has been in Tibetan Buddhism, to the best of my own limited capacity I have studied a variety of Buddhist texts and conferred with Tibetan lamas about end-of-life practices. I have studied *The Tibetan Book of the Dead* and its commentaries, which describe the intricate details of the stages of death and the in-between state, called *bardo*, between this life and the next. I have taken initiations into certain Tantras that

teach chants, prayers, visualizations, and psychic methods to prepare for and employ at the time of death. My teachers and readings
have taught me about the meditative techniques of Tibetan Yogis
who brought themselves to the point of death while meditating on
emptiness and compassion in order to transform themselves into
a bodily manifestation of a Buddha. I have been introduced to the
Tibetan practice called *powa*, where, at the time of death, the adept
concentrates his or her entire consciousness into the center of the
heart chakra. Then, at the time of death, through powerful visualizations, prayers, and mantras, their subtle core consciousness rises
up through the central channel, departs through the crown chakra
at the top of the head, and then manifests itself as a deity residing
in the heaven of the Buddha Amitaba.

Tibetan Buddhists share a belief with other major world religions that consciousness, at the last moment of life, is encompassed
in a magnificent clear light. At this moment, our consciousness
is not cluttered by all the emotions, sense objects, ideas, and dis-
tractions of normal life. It is free of worldly concerns and has
its greatest potential to directly perceive the ultimate truth, to
achieve perfect compassion, and to attain enlightenment. Therefore, one of the goals of spiritual practice is to prepare for this
moment so that we can use it fully. This final clear light moment
of death is a moment to be looked forward to and prepared for
as the culmination of a life of spiritual practice. *(See Joan Halifax's*
The Dissolution of the Body Meditation *on page 194).*

A NEW RESOLVE

So as I sat cross-legged on the end of my hospital bed that night
talking to my friend Bob about the bee sting, I was completely

deflated. After so much Buddhist training, I had nearly died, and I had no control over the circumstances, having fallen into a state that could be technically and accurately described as totally "unconscious."

But I was also still worried. I had begun to feel a sharp pain in my chest, right in the center of my sternum. I told the doctor about this, but he had no explanation. The pain persisted as Bob took me back to his house for the night where he and his wife, Ivy, served me tea and tucked me into a soft bed. The next day, Bob took me home to survey the scene of my "death" and to rest. As I lay down on the couch, Hunter suddenly appeared at my door and came in to see how I was doing. He carried a bouquet of flowers and some sweets, and we just sat and talked for about an hour. When I described the pain in my sternum, he began to laugh and told me about how he had tried to bring me back to life by giving me mouth-to-mouth resuscitation and by pounding on my chest with his fist. "God damn it," he said. "I wasn't going to let you go. Thank God the ambulance got here so quickly. They said you had no pulse, and we were very lucky to bring you back to life."

I lay there on the couch for the rest of the day, shocked by what had happened and feeling very lucky to be alive. But more than anything else, I resolved to be more prepared the next time death came knocking on my door. It was clear to me that I had more work to do in this life, and I redoubled my efforts to get it done.

SPIRITUAL PATHS AND THE LIVING-FULLY SEMINAR

Before this experience, I had what might be called an abstract interest in getting ready for death, and had occasionally talked to my teachers about it, asking if they would teach me something of the esoteric aspects of the end of life. And I think they did teach me these things anecdotally, but we never really got into it in a serious way. This was partly because of language issues and partly because of their conservative attitude toward transmission. But after I was stung by the bee, as far as I was concerned, there was no time to lose. Like an alcoholic who ends up in jail or the hospital before he learns to change his habits, I now knew I needed to have the doorway of death opened before me in order to see the fallacy in my self-image . . . and to make a change in my life. I needed to adapt to a new way of being, to invite more people to share in my life, enabling me to realize a vision I was having of a new spiritual network of cooperative learning and realization. I sold my business and began to reorganize my life toward realizing these goals.

In the early 1980s, Father Thomas Keating, one of the founders of the Centering Prayer movement and one of the great teachers of our time, began inviting spiritual leaders from many different religious traditions to a contemplative retreat at St. Benedict's Monastery in Snowmass, Colorado (described in the book, *The Common Heart: An Experience of Interreligious Dialogue*, 2006). There they would sit together in meditation and enter into deep dialogue about their respective spiritual practices and experiences. In 1998, Father Thomas invited me to join this group as a Buddhist representative, and it was there that I first learned of the extraordinary commonalities shared by many of the great contemplative traditions, especially by their mature practitioners. Through our meditations together, I also became aware of a kind of "InterSpiritual consciousness" emerging from these meditations in shared time, space, and silence. I learned how experiencing and dialoging about one another's distinctive practices could help each of us to deepen our own individual spiritual practice.

By working with Father Thomas and exemplars from other traditions, I began to see that the religions of the world were not isolated institutions, but interdependent phenomena within a vast spiritual ecosystem. This revelation led me to envision the Spiritual Paths Foundation and the Spiritual Paths Institute.

Taking a nonsectarian approach, I wanted to create an environment for individuals to collaborate in a process of spiritual inquiry and education about their respective contemplative practices. This I hoped would lead people to genuine insights about their own spiritual paths and help provide them with the resources to achieve a new level of understanding and integration of diverse spiritual paths. At the same time, I hoped to be able to engender a healthy respect and appreciation for both the diversity and the commonalities found in the world's spiritual traditions.

In 2000, I began to work in earnest to build the Spiritual Paths Foundation, seeking the wisdom and advice of spiritual elders like Father Thomas, Geshe Sopa, and Rabbi Zalman Schachter-Shalomi. I also set about building a unique Internet-based resource to facilitate the seeker's inquiry and created the first offerings of the Spiritual Paths Institute, a series of interspiritual seminars for the public.

These seminars were modeled on the kind of dialogue I had witnessed as a member of Father Thomas's Snowmass Conference. To each seminar I invited exemplars from the world's great spiritual traditions to spend several days together. In the course of those days, we would eat and talk together, form friendships, and begin a private dialogue that would culminate in a public seminar. At the seminar, each exemplar would give his or her own perspectives on the particular seminar topic and later participate in a focused interspiritual dialogue before an audience. After the audience had heard all the speakers, they were then given the opportunity in a smaller group setting to ask questions of the speaker who had touched them most. In this way, we could explore one topic from many different spiritual perspectives and in a very personal way.

We held our first Spiritual Paths seminar, The Way of Contemplation and Meditation, in 2002, and over the next year and a half, we held four more seminars on different topics in Colorado, New York, and California.[2] But, for the summer of 2004, I began work on something a little different and more personal to me. When we first started the foundation, one of the topics I most wanted to focus on—because of my own experiences, and because I felt it was important for our audience—was the end of life. But I didn't have the confidence to do it on my own; I didn't feel authentic about doing it, because I wasn't really doing that work professionally for other people. However, I was impressed by the work that my friend Tina Staley, then director of the Cancer Guide Program at Aspen Valley Hospital,[3] was doing, and I thought that she would be a good partner. She would bring an authenticity of working with people day-to-day who were dying, and I could bring a variety of spiritual perspectives to it. So Tina and I (and later Marilyn Schlitz of the Institute of Noetic Sciences) began to collaborate on a seminar to be called Living Fully: Preparing for the End of Life and Beyond.

It was very important for me to do this seminar well, so I threw myself into the subject, reading book after book and soliciting advice from numerous experts. But it wasn't enough to simply look at it abstractly; if I was going to create a meaningful program for other people, I had to put myself in their shoes and be willing to ask the questions that they might want to ask, and even those that they might not be ready to ask of themselves. I had to be willing to ask all of those questions of myself, and I didn't always like the answers I received.

Right away, we decided to go beyond a simple selection of spiritual teachers (as I had done in my other programs) to also gather renowned experts from the medical field, scientists, and philosophers to demonstrate how the integration of medicine, spirituality, philosophy, and science can lead to a positive, fulfilling, and transformative end-of-life experience.

The seminar finally took place over a beautiful weekend in July 2004 in Aspen, Colorado, and featured some of the most respected and innovative thinkers in the United States: Rabbi Zalman Schachter-Shalomi, a Hasidic rebbe and the founder of the Jewish Renewal and Spiritual Eldering movements; Joan Halifax Roshi, an expert on care for the dying and Shamanism, and a Zen abbess; Mother Tessa Bielecki, cofounder of the Spiritual Life Institute and a Carmelite Christian abbess; Dr. Ira Byock, bestselling author and one of the world's foremost authorities on palliative care; Dr. Marilyn Schlitz, vice president for Research and Education at the Institute of Noetic Sciences; William Cathers, a student of Mortimer Adler and a public philosopher; as well as Tina Staley and myself. The idea was that no matter where you were coming from or what your question was, there would be someone to address both you and it. We wanted to look at the questions of dying and the afterlife from as many perspectives as possible, and hopefully to begin to illustrate how combining these disciplines and perspectives might enable us to live each moment until the last with gratitude, vitality, and compassion, while also imparting a wisdom to help our family, friends, and colleagues go on without us.

It was a successful weekend for everybody involved. The talks went in unexpected directions, ideas were challenged, people were inspired, and the weekend was capped off by a remarkably inspiring and beautiful interspiritual service atop Aspen Mountain led by Reb Zalman, Mother Tessa, and Joan Halifax. It was one of our most successful programs and one of the most meaningful for me personally.

Just seven months later, I had my second brush with death.

THE PRACTICUM

Personally, the "Living-Fully" program was a way for me to develop my own perspectives on the end of life so that I would be better ready to die the next time. I just didn't know that it would happen so soon. That December I was cross-country skiing with friends John and Janie Bennett in Ashcroft above Aspen, when I had a very simple fall. It was nothing spectacular; I simply fell and landed on something hard, breaking my femur near the hip. I was transported out of the backcountry to the hospital where I had surgery. Eventually, I was released from the hospital, but without receiving proper instructions about taking a blood thinner. So when I drove out to California in early February 2005 for our Spiritual Paths program at La Casa de Maria in Santa Barbara called The Way of Contemplation and Compassionate Action, I was still on crutches and wasn't on a blood thinner. Sitting in a car for long periods with my feet and legs at that angle where clots can form if you are predisposed to them—*say, because of an operation*—was a big mistake.

By the time we started our program I wasn't feeling very well.

On Friday night, I introduced Father Thomas Keating, whom I credited as the inspiration behind Spiritual Paths. I told the audience how deeply Father Thomas's approach to interspirituality had affected my own spiritual development, and how my own deep meditation with his colleagues from many spiritual traditions had given me experiential courage to begin this project. The next morning, we all gathered for breakfast and then went into the main hall to begin our morning program. As I walked up to the podium to introduce Rabbi Rami Shapiro, I was suddenly stricken by a sharp and unrelenting pain in my chest, so excruciating that I could barely get a breath. I walked back out of the hall where I met Juliet, the program director for La Casa de Maria, who drove me back to the house where I was staying, then called the ambulance that whisked me off to the hospital.

The emergency room doctor, with the help of a CAT scan, soon diagnosed a pulmonary embolism. He told me that I had a number of blood clots in my lungs and then told me bluntly, "This could be fatal." If one of these clots were to lodge in the wrong place, I would die immediately, and there would be nothing medicine could do to save me. The staff began pumping morphine into my veins to relieve the pain, and the doctor ordered them to get me on blood thinner immediately.

I stayed in the hospital for several days as they tried to get my blood to the point that no more clots would develop. Occasionally, during the weekend, I would get a visit from Juliet and a phone call from the teachers telling me how things were going. Late Sunday afternoon, Father Keating, Rabbi Shapiro, Kabir and Camille Helminski, and the Venerable Tenzin Priyadarshi all came to the hospital room to see me. Truly, having each of these great spiritual exemplars together with me under these conditions was one of the most touching moments of my life. Even now, it brings tears to my eyes to remember their collective faces gathered around me in my hospital room.

On Monday, the hospital released me with a prescription for syringes of Lovenox, a blood thinner that I would inject into my stomach twice a day for a couple of weeks while another blood thinner, Coumadin, thinned my blood to the right level. The Sisters of the Immaculate Heart of Mary, who are the caretakers of La Casa de Maria, took me back into the Center for Spiritual Renewal, where I could rest and begin my recuperation. They also helped me to accept the need to relax into my weakened condition, to learn from it, and to make changes in my life that were now apparent and necessary. I began to realize just how much more of the illusion of control I needed to shed in my life, how much of my work I needed to release, and how sincerely I needed to ask for the help of others.

When I returned from the hospital, I was clearly in a weakened state. It was a new experience for me not to feel like the archetypal strong, protecting, providing male. Clearly, I was going through a major shift in my mode of being. The Sisters intuitively understood this and provided a safe place for my life transition as they settled me into a large bedroom that just a few days ago had been occupied by Father Thomas Keating (and years earlier by Thomas Merton). The room, enclosed by thick stone walls, spoke of the wealth of its original owners and occupants, yet it was subdued and unpretentious—a writing desk beneath the corner windows, a chair for reading, a bureau for clothing, and a long table with a glass statue of Mary (that mysteriously turned to face me during the night).

After a couple of days of convalescence, I awoke at about 1:30 a.m. on Wednesday morning with discomfort and some pain in my chest. It was not as severe as before, but it convinced me of the distinct possibility of another pulmonary emergency . . . and the possibility that I might die at any moment. The doctors had told me that this could be a killer and that it could happen immediately, without warning. So the imminence of death seemed very real.

It is curious to me now to reflect on my reactions to this episode. Strangely, I was not afraid anymore, yet I felt the urgency to prepare for imminent death. I felt that I had work to do and that I had to get to it without distraction or holding back. First, I wrote out instructions for the person who might find me dead. I told them who to call, how to handle my body, how I would like the memorial service and cremation, and where to scatter my ashes. I left some words of advice and expressions of love to my children, Jonathan and Alexandra, my mother, Ann, and my sister, Marianne.

Then I spent the rest of the night in meditation and prayer. I did not want to sleep through my death. I wanted to be present and fully conscious, full of compassion, and meditating on emptiness. I wanted to be centered in the core of my heart chakra, to consciously manifest myself in the form of a *bodhisattva* who, in the next life, could compassionately help countless beings achieve liberation of enlightenment. I prayed to the divine consciousness within and around us to help guide me through the experiences between this life and the next, and to make me an instrument of divine compassion and wisdom in the next life. I imagined the confusion and fear that might accompany my death and vowed to keep my spiritual focus and intention no matter what might distract me (as advised in *The Tibetan Book of the Dead*). In my meditation, I developed a tranquil, one-pointed focus that would sustain me during the dreamlike stages between this life and the next. I prepared myself to experience an all-encompassing clear, white light, and vowed that at that moment my consciousness would become enlightened for the sake of all beings.

That night I was prepared to die. I had been preparing for this night ever since my "death" by bee sting and, it seems, many years before that. After five hours of writing, meditating, and praying, the sun rose in the east, and I was still alive. I had lived through the night and the many nights that followed, and I am now deeply grateful for this opportunity to rehearse the moment of my death. This predeath experience was a kind of practicum where I could try to put into service my years of training and preparation.

GIVING BACK AND LIVING FULLY

During those several nights in which I did not expect to wake again, a new appreciation for life was created in me, something oddly akin to being in love. And over the next couple of weeks, I both experienced and observed how I was releasing more and more of my old sense of self. I became less and less attached to the qualities with which I had previously defined myself; I gave up the illusion that I could or should be in control of my life, relationships, and work; I became more and more present in each moment; I felt compassion and love for everyone I met and talked with; I stopped judging their personalities, habits, bodies, and careers. I seem to have been experiencing and witnessing the meaning of the great Sufi mantra, "Die before you die." I was aware of how many aspects of my life were dying and that this kind of dying is more profound than the mere death of the physical body. Father Thomas calls this "the death of the false self," the elimination of the false and useless aspects of our being that are simply addicted to unhealthy habits, emotions, and concepts of reality. If we can truly *die before we die*, we can shed all this dross and be freed to live our life fully without the shackles of normal human existence.

Of course, in time the old habits began to reassert themselves, but I am mindful of them now (they don't have the same habitual force), and I can honestly say I will never be the same. The first near-death experience had shifted something inside me, as had the transformative seminar Tina Staley and I had organized in Aspen. I learned so much from our teachers at the seminar and from simply preparing for it, that when death came knocking a second time, the situation was different, and so was I.

Even so, there are questions that have remained for me. What does it mean to prepare for a conscious dying process when, in fact, you may have no control whatsoever, as with my bee sting? That situation has not changed. It could happen to any one of us without warning. And why would my friend Hunter Thompson fight so hard for my life and not his own eight years later?

Hunter and I had been friends for over thirty-five years. We had met back in the halcyon days when we both had the hubris to believe that we would change the world. They were heady, fun, frivolous, and yet also earnest times. I helped him manage his campaign for sheriff and spent many hours plotting local politics and reading back to him the pearls of his early Gonzo journalism that so emboldened the minds of several generations. While I was in California breathing life back into my own clot-strewn lungs, he had left me a telephone message, less than an hour before he committed suicide with a bullet through his head, to come to his house for some conversation and "a little shooting." Of course, I wondered if things would have been different if I would have been home and present for him.

But what these last two questions really come down to is living fully: What does it mean to live fully? And can we do it if we have not come to terms with death and the dying process? Thus, the dialogue and resources in this book deal with four basic aspects of living fully and dying well, and the questions that go with them:

> *Living*—How does an understanding of the process of dying help us to engage fully in our own life with meaning, purpose, and contentment? What examples and stories can help us to grasp this? How can I live my life in this way? How can I joyfully live my life in preparation for death? What meditations, prayers, mantras, visualizations, perspectives, and attitudes should I learn and develop now so that I am ready for death at any moment?

> *Dying*—The process of dying can be instant or it can last for hours, days, weeks, months, or years. What are the predictable stages of the dying process? How can we prepare for this? What tools and techniques can we acquire so that we can be content and purposeful in the dying process? How should we positively prepare and engage our family and friends in our dying process—psychologically, spiritually, emotionally, physically? How and when should we organize our living will,

insurance, finances, possessions, businesses, and so on to prepare for the inevitable, yet uncertain time of our dying process? How should I plan for my own care if my death is slow, expensive, and painful? How should I involve family and friends? What are the options for helping me through the dying process, including spiritual guides, psychological counseling, treatment guides, assisted living, intensive care, home care, and hospice? How can I help my friends and loved ones in their process of dying?

Death—What is death? Is death the final act of our existence? Is death a process of transformation to another form of life? What happens when we die? What are the stages of death physically, emotionally, and intellectually? How can death become a meaningful, purposeful, transformative experience? How can we be aware and conscious of dying and guide ourselves through it? How can we avoid fear and mental anguish? How can we do it with purpose and contentment?

Beyond—What do the world's spiritual traditions say about life beyond death? What is the philosophical rationale for life after death? What are the credible reports from both individuals and medical research about continued existence? How can I have knowledge and faith that I will continue to exist after my death? How would faith in an afterlife alter the way I live my present life? How

would my behavior and state of mind during my
life, dying, and death influence the form, place, and
quality of my continuing existence?

Of course, we cannot hope to answer these questions defini-
tively, but we can begin a conversation here that will address all
of the basic issues in one way or another. With the help of the
original participants in our Spiritual Paths seminar, we have at-
tempted to create a book that will provide you with a variety
of different perspectives—spiritual, medical, psychological, and
scientific—allowing you to craft for yourself an integrated intellectual understanding of dying and the afterlife. In addition, we
have brought together a number of valuable resources to help
you prepare, or to help others to proactively engage the dying
process as a positive and transformative experience.

DR. EDWARD W. BASTIAN
The sailing yacht Uma Karuna
Santa Barbara Harbor, California, 2009

Living Fully
Dying Well

PART I

Dialogue and Reflection on Living Fully and Dying Well

ONE

Coming to Terms
with Our Mortality

*Is death something so terrible and absurd that we are
better off not thinking or talking about it? . . . Or is it
possible to befriend our dying gradually and live open to
it, trusting that we have nothing to fear? Is it possible to
prepare for our death with the same attentiveness that our
parents had in preparing for our birth? Can we wait for
our death as for a friend who wants to welcome us home?*

HENRI J. M. NOUWEN
Our Greatest Gift: A Meditation on Dying and Caring

I n the pages that follow, Dr. Edward W. Bastian, founder of
the Spiritual Paths Foundation, talks with both Joan Halifax
Roshi and Rabbi Zalman Schachter-Shalomi about the difficulties of facing our own mortality. Joan is the founder of the
Project on Being with Dying, training health-care professionals

in contemplative care of the dying, and the author of *Being with Dying: Cultivating Compassion and Fearlessness in the Presence of Death*. Zalman Schachter-Shalomi, better known as Reb Zalman, is the founder of the Spiritual Eldering movement and the author of *From Age-ing to Sage-ing: A Profound New Vision of Growing Older*. They discuss questions of facing the best- and worst-case scenarios of our own death to confront our fears head on, rather than avoiding them.   — *Ed.*

DR. EDWARD W. BASTIAN There is a popular book by Stephen and Ondrea Levine called *Who Dies?*[1] And I think it's a great question for us (even outside of its rhetorical Buddhist context), because death is so often the proverbial "elephant in the room." Nobody wants to talk about it; all of us will experience infirmity, aging, and the irresistible "mystery of death," but we live as if death is something that only happens to other people. So perhaps we should begin with, "Who dies?"

JOAN HALIFAX ROSHI Robert Thurman likes to say, "We all have a sexually transmitted terminal condition. It's called being human."[2] It's funny when you hear it that way, but it gets the point across.

Sometimes I like to begin a talk on dying with an experiment. I ask a series of questions and request that the people stand up if the question applies to them. After they stand up, I thank them, and they sit down again. First, I start with people in health care . . . doctors, nurses, people who work in nursing homes or for hospice. Then I ask people to stand who are currently taking care of a dying person, those who have lost a good friend or a family member, those who have lost a child, and those who have had a catastrophic illness in the past or currently have a catastrophic illness. And by this time most of the audience has risen at least once and participated in a living demographic, seeing people stand up alone or in clusters all around the room. Then I ask, "Those of you who have 'issues' around your mortality, around death, will you please stand up?" And for this last question, everyone, or nearly everyone stands. Then I ask my final question, "Those of you who want to die in a hospital, will you please stand up?" *No one stands.*[3]

I have asked these last two questions of thousands and thousands of people, and the response is uniform: we have "issues" with our mortality, and we are afraid of dying in a hospital. And the thing we have to know is that most of us will die in a hospital at this point in our society! Personally, I would really like excellent care when I die, and a hospital offers that possibility. But it's a revolution in consciousness, and a revolution in society, that we're asking for; we need it for ourselves, our children, our parents, and our grandparents.

DR. EDWARD W. BASTIAN It really seems to me that these two issues could be boiled down to . . . *fear of death* and *fear of dying.* One seems to be a problem with the unknown, and the other with the known, what we know enough about to fear—murder, tragic accidents, catastrophic illnesses, and the dreaded hospital. How can we get past these fears? Reb Zalman?

RABBI ZALMAN SCHACHTER-SHALOMI You know, at this point, I am over eighty years old, and there is a certain truth that one speaks when one gets close to the end of life. And so what I have to say is as much a "witness" as they are ideas.

There is a lot about death that is painful and that gives us grief—violent death and catastrophic illness, people being snatched up in the midst of their lives — and these often cause us to think of death as something we have to escape; that's the "emergency room" mentality, where you save a life at any cost. But there is another death about which the Bible speaks when it says, "he was old and sated with days."[4] And there is that wonderful promise in the Psalms, saying, "with length of days I will satisfy you,"[5] so that when we get to that ending moment, we can look back at life and say, paraphrasing Goldilocks and the Three Bears, "not too long, not too short . . . just right." *(See Zalman Schachter-Shalomi's "Life Review Exercises" on pages 153–160.)*

Without forgetting the tragedies of lives being lost everywhere in our world, the people dying from AIDS and other diseases, and the compassion that we need to have for our Mother, the planet, who is crying out from all the pain that she is experiencing now, we need to learn to talk about what is "just right," to talk about the kind of death where one is *sated with days,* and of what happens to us after we leave the body.

DR. EDWARD W. BASTIAN Will you start us off on that conversation?

RABBI ZALMAN SCHACHTER-SHALOMI First, we have to talk about what is holding us back. The truth is, we are not usually very sophisticated about the feelings that are going on with us. For instance, many of us have had — at some point in our lives — an experience of feeling "That's *it,* I'm gone." Whether, God forbid, when you had an automobile accident or an illness, something caused you to ask with your feelings, often in an instant, *"Is this it?"* But notice how when you try to go back to that moment, trying to remember the feeling of *"Is this it?"* just how quickly you switch gears from *feeling* to *thinking* and abstraction; most of the time, you'll hardly be aware a switch has happened!

In a way, we are "hardwired" not to spend time with that feeling. The earliest and most basic brain construct known to us is what is called the "reptilian brain."[6] And while our brains have evolved much more sophistication over time, the reptilian aspect of the brain is still functioning. So when you sense danger or experience fear of the unknown, the adrenaline starts pumping and everything in your body gets organized for a "fight or flight" response. But if when the feeling of *"Is this it?"* comes up, we can keep from reacting with the reptilian brain—if we can take a breath and say, "What else is there?"—then we can learn something about transitioning out of this life.

DR. EDWARD W. BASTIAN If the reptilian brain is counterproductive here, then what aspect of the brain allows us to take that "breath" and become comfortable with the idea of facing our mortality?

RABBI ZALMAN SCHACHTER-SHALOMI For this, we have to use the "limbic brain," the aspect of our brain that can reach out and be cozy with these feelings, allowing us to stick around and settle into *"Is this it?"* From that settledness, we can move into the cortex, which wants to understand, "What was my life all about?" and then, move still further beyond the cortex to the place where we can ask with curiosity as we approach death, "What is this *momentous* feeling all about? What happens beyond that 'door'?" *(See Zalman Schachter-Shalomi's "Exercises for Facing Our Mortality" on pages 161–169.)*

Of course, the reptilian brain chimes in again at this point, asking, "Do you want to be distracted from that now?" And the answer is, "No, I don't want to be distracted; I know that the inevitable is about to come, and I don't want to fight it. I want to surrender to it. I want to relax into it." And in this feeling of peaceful resignation, you can say "amen" to the long hymn of life.

DR. EDWARD W. BASTIAN The fear response of the reptilian brain is interesting here, because usually we get carried away with "worst-case scenarios" and our desire to control the circumstances; what can we do when we are already into that response?

JOAN HALIFAX ROSHI We can use it. I often ask people to explore the "worst-case scenario" in their imagination, touching into the details, seeing who is there, looking at all the circumstances, and paying attention to how old they are in that scenario; because often this fear is just under the skin of your heart and ends up shaping a lot of your decisions. So I think it's worthwhile to take a close look at just what you are afraid of—what thoughts and feelings come up for you as you explore this scenario—and to look at how the body feels. Just to take notice of them, and notice if you don't want to go there, as Reb Zalman was saying.

Once you've done that, then it is important to look at your "best-case scenario"; how do you really want to die? What do you want to die of? Whom do you want to be there? When? Where? And again, notice your thoughts and feelings and how your body feels as you explore that scenario. When that is coming through clearly, you should ask yourself, "What do I need to give away, and what do I need to do to enhance the possibility of my best-case scenario? What are my priorities? What's really important in terms of how I live and how I die?" *(See Zalman*

Schachter-Shalomi's Scripting Our Last Moments on Earth *in "Exercises for Facing Our Mortality" on page 164.)*

My own answers to these questions have changed a lot over the years. So it's really important for us to continue exploring these questions, because all of us will face decisions related to our health care and the health care of others sooner or later.

Death is often seen as simply a physiological event, and some even view it as a failure, and even in some instances, a kind of moral failure . . . the ultimate defeat. But the truth is, death is a developmental phase in our life cycle.

DR. EDWARD W. BASTIAN What is the benefit of bringing this knowledge into our awareness?

RABBI ZALMAN SCHACHTER-SHALOMI Elisabeth Kübler-Ross[7] once described how one of her patients said to her, *Ich will mein Sterben erleben,* "I want to live through my dying." They didn't want to sleep through it; not like Woody Allen, when he says, "I don't mind dying as long as I don't have to be there!" On the contrary, I want to be there!

Coming to terms with one's mortality is important work, especially for elders today; if we, as elders, don't come to terms with our mortality, we aren't going to do the eldering work that is necessary for the health of the planet. We'll just "get old," wasting years in a protracted dying, "killing time" while we could be living and giving what we know back to the planet. *(See Zalman Schachter-Shalomi's* A Voice for the Planet *in "Exercises for Facing Our Mortality" on page 168.)*

The Earth needs elder-mind today as much as She ever did. It has always been the task of elders to give over wisdom to the next generation, to be wisdom keepers and to pass that wisdom and experience on to others. It is really important that we grow into sages, that we grow into elderhood with wisdom. We have to realize—yes, technology is changing rapidly, information is increasing exponentially, but how to use it responsibly *is not*— responsibility needs wisdom, not more information. That wisdom comes from sages, from people who are seasoned with a life full of deep experience. But "age-ing" only becomes "sage-ing" as we come to terms with our own mortality, as we take account of our lives and temper our experiences against the knowledge of our eventual death.[8]

TWO

A Life of Deaths, and More Life!

If we cannot face death, then we cannot face life and fall prone to life-failure.

We desperately want to live. But we cannot face life without facing death. When we refuse, we become sick and neurotic. Instead of suffering life to the point of death, we repress in sophisticated ways and keep death, and therefore new life, at a distance. We talk about life and analyze it but don't live because we cannot endure the deaths it takes to come magnificently alive. We avoid the parlous adventure of life, the shame of the cross, and the ineluctable fact of death in every genuine "I-Thou" relationship, in every soulful act of love. We keep "cuddling up" to persons and institutions, escaping the reality of death in cozy little huddles: in comfortable churches, petrifying prayer groups, and massive religious crusades. . . . There is only one gateway to freedom and openness to the Ultimate, to infinite possibilities or finite impossibilities; that gateway is death. There is no new life without death of the old.

*We need to begin with the death of the empirical
separative ego and the ego's world. . . . Death, as the ultimate
breakthrough of our life, must involve a kind of violence —
a wild human passion — if our proud self-imprisonment
is to be broken open. We prepare for the final act of death
which will usher us into eternal life by striking mortal
blows now to the false self, to the grasping, craving ego.
Encountering death isn't the same as being in the danger
of death. Having a rope around your neck may not be as
salvific as watching a leaf fall from a tree in autumn or
burning a letter from your lover or selling your motorcycle.*

WILLIAM MCNAMARA, O.C.D.
Christian Mysticism: The Art of the Inner Way

PRAYER

AFTER I SOLD my business in 1999, I had two cases of
pneumonia within a year. On both occasions, I was in bed
for over a month. During those extended periods, I was
willing to do a lot of experimenting with how I could help
my lungs heal — psychological experiments dealing with
grief, with emotional traumas related to the lungs — in addition to getting proper medical treatment. The second
time I got very sick, the doctor told me I should be in the
hospital. But I had been doing so much spiritual work that
I didn't want to go into a hospital and "give it away" to a
doctor; I felt I was getting to some place of honesty in my
own practice that I had never gotten to before.

So it was a Saturday night, and I was lying in bed, and I got really scared because I was having a hard time breathing. I called the doctor, who said, "Get to the hospital." But I said to myself, "What are you going to do?" And then it came to me; in all my years of practicing Buddhism, the one thing that has not been a part of my practice is prayer. It was a revelation, because I was a Buddhist following a Buddhist path, doing the practices with a heavy emphasis on personal responsibility. And somehow I thought that by doing these practices I was "in charge" of my spiritual destiny! But that night, as I was lying there in fear, I said, "Man, you gotta pray! You need help, and you cannot do this on your own!" And so the question came up for me, "Well, *what* am I going to pray to? I don't believe in God, so what am I going to pray to?" Soon the answer came up, "You're going to pray to that aspect of your Infinite Consciousness that is capable of healing and being healed, and that is also listening and sensitive . . . *Compassion.*" So I went into an hour or two of deep prayer, and then I fell asleep, and when I woke in the morning, I was on the road to recovery.

DR. EDWARD W. BASTIAN

I n the pages that follow, Dr. Edward W. Bastian talks with Tessa Bielecki and Rabbi Zalman Schachter-Shalomi about what Bielecki calls the "daily dying" and the "life failure" that may occur if we do not engage death consciously. Tessa

Bielecki is a Carmelite Christian hermit and former abbess of the Spiritual Life Institute. She is the author of *Teresa of Avila: Ecstasy and Common Sense.* Rabbi Zalman Schachter-Shalomi demonstrates here why he is well known as an adept in interspiritual dialogue and spiritual counseling. They address questions such as: Can we live fully when we fear death? Can having "little deaths" throughout life help us when we encounter death itself? —*Ed.*

DR. EDWARD W. BASTIAN My own brushes with death have really made me question deeply those parts of myself that I have to let die. A sense of "control" is one of them. But when I really begin to think about this, it occurs to me that from a certain perspective our whole life seems like a series of momentary deaths, a continual process of dying, of letting go; could we not use these "momentary deaths" to help prepare us for the "big death"?

TESSA BIELECKI One of the most important teachings I've received is this: "Choose death now, and draw from that confrontation consequences for a life fully lived."[1] The point is, the confrontation with death is coming at us all the time, and we need to be awake enough to respond to it.

DR. EDWARD W. BASTIAN What does it mean to "choose death now"?

TESSA BIELECKI It is my experience that people do not experience "resurrection" enough because they don't let themselves *die dead enough.* We begin to die and it is so terrifying, or so uncomfortable, so awful, that we pull back from the experience. And so we don't experience the resurrection; we don't experience all the life that is waiting for us because we don't have the courage to die. So that is one way to look at "choosing death."

DR. EDWARD W. BASTIAN We don't allow ourselves to live fully because we don't allow ourselves to "die dead enough"? And you are speaking of the "false self" that we need to let die?

TESSA BIELECKI Yes . . . another way to look at it is through the lens we were using just a moment ago, that we live "a life of deaths," that is, we go through a continual process of letting go. These are what I call the "little deaths," and many of the most significant moments in my life have come as a result of these.

DR. EDWARD W. BASTIAN Would you be willing to share some of these "little deaths"?

TESSA BIELECKI The first of the "little deaths" that comes to mind is the death of loved ones. I have lost a great many loved ones in my life: my eight-year-old brother died of leukemia; and six months to the day after that, my sixteen-year-old brother was killed in an automobile accident. I was eighteen at the time, and our family was never the same . . . my mother, especially.

As I reflected on this over the years, I realized my mother died emotionally in that second death. I know now from my grief work that the loss of a child is the most terrible loss anyone can suffer. This was over forty years ago, and at that time there were not a lot of resources for helping people through grief. My parents didn't get help. So in a very real way, the kind of family life that we had been living died too. It was more than losing two brothers; I also lost my mother then, and we lost our family's way of life.

DR. EDWARD W. BASTIAN The "little deaths" and dyings are about loss and a gradual letting go?

TESSA BIELECKI Yes, and there is no limit to the forms they may take. Some of my most painful losses have even been of places . . . the "death of places." I have built *and lost* two monasteries in my life. We started out in Sedona, Arizona, and if you know anything about Arizona, you know it is a harsh environment. When we had to leave that monastery after twenty years, I had to leave a garden that I had literally poured my youth into creating. I had to leave the soil. If you're a gardener, and you have had to garden in a harsh place, and you have built up soil from nothing, and you have to leave that soil . . . believe me, it's a death. And it happened to me twice.

Our second monastery was in Nova Scotia, Canada. We had to leave there because of encroaching logging, and I had to lose a garden all over again after twenty-seven years. We were twenty years in Sedona, twenty-seven years in Nova Scotia. And once again, I had to wrench myself away from the soil. I had to leave the garden. For some that may sound like nothing, but for me, these deaths were terrible. It wasn't just the loss of the place, it was a loss of identity, the death of chapters in my life, the death of who I thought I was. And then you realize . . . "*no, that isn't who I am.*" (See Joan Halifax's Facing Loss *in "Practices for the Caregiver and the Bereaved" on page 225.*)

There are also the deaths that I call "daily dying." For me, a white peony is the most perfect creation that God has made. And I have planted a lot of peonies in my life and lost a lot of peony bushes as I've had to move. But I still remember the death of a single peony in my hermitage in Nova Scotia with particular poignancy. I had one exquisite symbol of all the perfection that is possible in life sitting on my desk . . . and right before my eyes, that peony dropped all its petals at once. Not one by one. Truthfully, I heard the noise as these delicate, light petals hit the desk . . . almost like thunder. I had to ask, how could anything so perfect pass away? That was a remarkably deep, enlightening experience for me. St. Teresa of Avila teaches, "All things pass. God never changes. . . . God alone suffices, *solo Dios basta*."

DR. EDWARD W. BASTIAN Is that why we let go? To receive what "never changes," the one thing that "alone suffices"?

TESSA BIELECKI As a Christian, I say it this way: we are letting go of life for the sake of *more life*. Because I'm a Catholic and not a Protestant I cannot quote biblical texts by chapter and verse, except for one, which is my favorite, and which for me sums up the essence of Christianity: "I have come that you may have life and have it to the full." John 10:10.

Christianity is about *life*. St. Teresa of Avila says, "O death, death, I don't know who fears you, since life lies in you!"[2]

Now, I would say many, if not most, people do not experience the Christian tradition as the giver of life. But I have been very blessed and have received life and more life for more than sixty years. So that is the essence of it for me. "I have come that you may have life and have it to the full."

That is the central mystery of Christianity, what we call the Paschal Mystery, the Passover Mystery . . . the passover from death into new life, which is usually depicted in the crucifixion of Jesus. I do not see *only* death in a crucifix. Resurrection images can be very difficult to portray. The resurrection is much more mysterious and is much more than the body, so how do you portray that? When I look at a crucifix, I don't see "death" so much as I see the whole mystery of dying into life, letting go of life for the sake of more life. If you make a compost pit—and I happen to be a fiend for making compost!—this is a very real way of meditating on exactly what I'm talking about.

The "daily dying" is also a part of my lifestyle as a Christian monk.[3] Monks take vows of *poverty, chastity, and obedience,* and through these vows we practice dying on a daily basis.

Death strips us of all external possessions; we anticipate this stripping by being content with life's essentials and nothing superfluous (poverty). Death deprives us of our biological vitality; we anticipate this by renouncing lust, the sexual obsessions of our culture, and exploiting others for our own gratification (chastity). Death means the end of our pretended independence; we shed such pretenses by "listening" to the voices of others in our world and living interdependently (obedience, from the Latin *oboedire,* "to listen").

According to William McNamara, there is no "better way of dying, or defeating the ego, than the practice of poverty, chastity, and obedience, which involve not principles of opposition to evil but expressions of a higher choice. The dynamic interplay of these virtues may be better understood if we translate these almost hackneyed words into their simplest and deepest meaning. Poverty means no fuss. Chastity means no lust. Obedience means no rust."

DR. EDWARD W. BASTIAN I have heard from Sufi[4] friends that we must die to the flesh, in a sense, in order to experience more of the life of the spirit, that is to say, deeper levels of intuition and subtle awareness;[5] would that not be a death for more life, or a fuller life in this world? Reb Zalman?

RABBI ZALMAN SCHACHTER-SHALOMI Yes, but we need to understand that what the Sufis are saying with this is not against the body — not a killing of the body — but a transcending of the belief that we are only a body of flesh. And with that comes more life, a fuller life experience, as Tessa was saying.

All of us — whether we are aware of it or not — live in unseen realities, in a holarchy[6] of organisms. One of these is our physical organism, our physical body. But, beyond that, there is also an energy body, an affect body, a mental body, and a spiritual body. The energy body is our field of magnetism, enveloping the physical body. The affect body is still greater and is formed of our feelings. Think of everyone you have cared for, whom you love, and who love you back — there is a connection to them, a togethering that happens with them — this was the original meaning of *ecclesia*, "a gathering of people," like-minded beings plugging into one another in feeling! And then, if you look to the mental body—that is to say, all that we share in mind with everyone else —can you imagine how many people are thinking similarly at this very moment, and how you are connected with all of them! That's a whole other life that we have! Then of course we go to the spiritual body. Here we are really together in every moment with the One who brings us into being. There is no two-ness in this place, just *One*. And we are alive on this level too.

When my sister was dying from cancer, she was having a very hard time of it. It was breast cancer, and it had spread all over her body, and she felt as if she would be forever locked into the painful body she was experiencing at that particular time. And when we talked about this and what it means to drive an old car to the junkyard and to get out before they crush it, she suddenly had such a sense of relief, knowing that she would no longer be a prisoner of that body. So when the time comes to scrap the body, the "old car," it is important to say, "This was simply my vehicle in this life. I *am* a soul, and I *have* a body, and that body is wearing out." Some of us may even say, "I'm already half a bionic person, you know — I've got dentures. I've got glasses. I need to use hearing aids — clearly, the body is wearing out. This body goes, but *I* am not finished yet." *(See Joan Halifax's* The Dissolution of the Body Meditation *in "Meditations and Preparation for the Moment of Death" on page 194.)*

When considering the end of life, we have to learn to say, "I am not my body. This body is worn out, but I have other organisms. I have a spiritual organism. I have a mental organism. I have an affective organism; only the physical organism is being discarded at this point. I am not dying just because I am giving up my body." The sooner you can make that distinction, the better. It is common in spiritual traditions to hear talk of death as "giving up the body"; sometimes it is talked about as "dropping the body," as if whatever was supporting it moved on. Hearing this, you get the sense of what it means when it is said, "What am I? I am a drop of the Divine Ocean." As the soul-drop flows back into the Ocean and becomes one with It, you might ask, "Am I diminished or enriched by that?"

Jalaluddin Rumi[7] has this wonderful sentiment: "I was born a stone and died a stone. I was resurrected as a plant and died as a plant. I was resurrected as an animal and died as an animal. I was resurrected as a human being and died as a human being. I was resurrected as an angel and died as an angel. And then I was resurrected in God. O death, where is thy sting, if by thy means I have gained so much?" Can you imagine a caterpillar saddened by its own transformation? And do you remember the sign that Elisabeth Kübler-Ross used for Shanti-Nilaya, her organization? It was a butterfly.[8]

But how do I know I will survive that moment when my body ceases to be? *By spending time in our other "bodies."* If you practice Yoga or Tai Chi, doing *pranayama*[9] work and moving *chi,*[10] you are already spending time in the energy body and may have even experienced it. These are bodies that we can tune ourselves into and raise our consciousness to; we "feel" the unique consciousness of these places and know the difference between one and another; having been there, we can know that they exist. You won't find the *kundalini*[11] in the gross anatomy lab, but you can experience it. By experiencing these other bodies, we learn to identify less with *only* the physical body, and this experience is very important for our encounter with the afterlife.

DR. EDWARD W. BASTIAN And if we continue to deny death? What then?

TESSA BIELECKI What results from the denial of death is "life failure." If we don't look at death, we don't know how to live. Again, William McNamara says, "We desperately want to live. But we cannot face life without facing death. When we refuse, we become sick and neurotic. Instead of suffering life to the point of death, we repress in sophisticated ways and keep death, and therefore new life, at a distance. We talk about life and analyze it but don't live because we cannot endure the deaths it takes to come magnificently alive. . . . There is no new life without death of the old."

DR. EDWARD W. BASTIAN And what can we do about the fear that keeps us from living fully?

TESSA BIELECKI For me it has been important to look at how Jesus approached his death, because, in his example, we find both deep peace and, at the same time, deep fear. He was so full of sorrow in his "agony in the garden," the night before his death, as we read in the Gospel of Matthew, "And sadness came over him, and great distress. Then he said to his disciples, 'My soul is sorrowful to the point of death' . . . he fell on his face and prayed. 'My Father,' he said, 'if it is possible, let this cup pass me by. Nevertheless, let it be as you, not I, would have it.'"[12] And looking at that, I say, "Well, if Jesus was afraid and sad, then there is certainly nothing the matter with me or anyone else being afraid." Nevertheless, in the end, Jesus went on to face his death humbly, heroically, and unafraid, as we see in the Christian saints and mystics who followed him.

I suspect that the fear has to do with the surface levels of the human being. On deeper levels, we can reach such a place where we are not afraid. I think of that beautiful passage from one of the Eastern Orthodox Christian saints, St. John Chrysostom, who has an incredibly eloquent way of describing how the resurrection of Jesus plays a trick on the devil, and Hell becomes a joke. It is an amazing way to look at this whole experience. St. Teresa says, "I die because I do not die." That's a *koan* for a lifetime, right there.

> No one needs to be afraid of death; for our Savior has
> died and set us free.
> He has confronted death in his own person and
> obliterated it.

He made it obsolete with the taste of his flesh.
This is what Isaiah foretold when he said:
"Hell stands in fear of the encounter with him."

Of course it is in fear.
For now Hell is laughable, a joke, and finished.
In fear because now taken prisoner.
It grabbed at a body and encountered God.
It swallowed the earth, but choked on Heaven.
It seized only what it saw, but was smashed by what it did
    not see.

Poor death, where is your sting?
Poor Hell, where is your triumph?
Christ rises from the tomb and you become nothing.
Christ rises and the angels are jubilant.
Christ rises and life is set free.
Christ rises and the graves are emptied of the dead.[13]

ST. JOHN CHRYSOSTOM

THREE

Care from
the Heart

*Some form of the denial of death can probably be found
in all cultures. But death is somehow different . . . in the
modern world.*

*On the one hand, we have medical and technological
means to forestall death's encroachment that were unimaginable
in previous ages. The development of these technologies require
us to give sustained attention to the unthinkable reality of
death. But what sort of attention does it require? Do we think
about death as a kind of mechanical problem to be solved? If
that is how we think about it, then we are not really thinking
about death. We are not thinking about our death, the death
whose breath we can feel on our neck if we turn our mind
to it for only a second; we are thinking about something
held at a safe distance and subjected to our scientific gaze.*

*The scientific gaze distances us from death, not only
because it gives us a mask of objectivity with which to
hide—even from ourselves—the terror that my death*

*inspires, but also because it allows me to think that my
objective distancing of death will somehow, some day, allow me
to defeat death. Death is approached not only as a problem
to be mastered, but as a problem that will be mastered. . . .*

*Perhaps death is unthinkable because it would force
us to think of ourselves as ultimately, finally, completely
without control.*

FREDERICK BAUERSCHMIDT
Why the Mystics Matter Now

A BETTER WAY

AS A CHILD I was very fortunate to have spent a lot of time
with my grandmother. She was a woman from Savannah,
Georgia, with hair so long she could stand on it. And as a
woman in Savannah, she had a very community-oriented
pattern of life, a role in society that was quite ordinary for
her, but which may seem extraordinary to us. You know,
women of that era, our grandmothers, many of them had
a very different relationship to caring for dying people
than we do. They just took it as part of their life. Death was
normalized. And women in a village or in a town (Savannah
wasn't such a huge town then) were very closely knit, and
people in that kind of town were taking care of each other
simply as part of their way of life.

When I was a little girl, I would go and stay with my
grandmother, and I got to sleep in my grandmother's bed.
So my grandmother would come back from taking care of
somebody who was dying, and I'd get into bed with her

and snuggle up to her, and then she'd tell me all about it. Death became normalized for me through the attitude of my grandmother. Not only that, my grandmother was a sculptress, and she made some of the most beautiful monuments in Bonaventure Cemetery in Savannah. To her, death was a way that she could serve a population that she really cared about.

Then she got colon cancer. And she was really strong through that—she just handled it. But then she also had a series of strokes. And this was at the time when death was being "medicalized." It was something that happened inside of an institution. And so my family was ignorant—wonderful people, but what did we know about what to do?—so we put her in a nursing home.

My grandmother had this deep wish to die. She knew death was okay, but she had no way to die herself. I remember sitting with her in this nursing home and her begging my father, saying, "John, help me die," with one side of her face all frozen. I still remember how her toes were curled, and how her toenails were untrimmed—as a young person, it made a very deep impression on me . . . her physical presence and appearance. "John, help me die." And my father, who was a wonderful person, would look at her and experience absolute helplessness. We all did. We didn't know how to take care of her at home.

So when my grandmother died, and she was in her coffin—it was a Savannah funeral, open coffin—and I went up and I sat with her, her face was at peace. I looked into her coffin, and I promised her, "I'm going to do something. You didn't deserve this. I'm so sorry. There's got to be a better way." And of course, there is.

JOAN HALIFAX ROSHI

I n the pages that follow, Dr. Edward W. Bastian talks with Dr. Ira Byock, Tina L. Staley, and Joan Halifax Roshi about how we approach death in our conventional health-care facilities and how we might change this approach for the better. Dr. Byock is the director of Palliative Medicine at Dartmouth Hitchcock Medical Center in Lebanon, New Hamsphire, and professor of Anesthesiology and Community and Family Medicine at Dartmouth Medical School. Tina L. Staley is the director of Pathfinders National and an Integrative Oncology instructor at Duke University Medical Center. Many of us fear dying in a hospital and being at the mercy of the health-care system. This discussion addresses issues such as, How can we work with this possibility of dying in a hospital or nursing home? How can we avoid demoralizing ourselves and others with this attitude? How can we promote ways to work within the system? — *Ed.*

DR. EDWARD W. BASTIAN I want to come back to something Joan said about hospitals and the "revolution" needed in health care. In the description of her experiment, it became abundantly clear that almost as great as our fear of death is our fear of dying in a hospital. All of us, I believe, are appreciative of the "miracles" of modern medicine, but I don't think it would be shocking to anyone if I suggested that this triumph has sometimes come at the expense of the person or the personal in health care. Perhaps we could talk a little bit about how this happened and what we can do to change it?

DR. IRA BYOCK Medicine is built on the twin human problems of illness and injury. Its goals are cure, life prolongation, restoration of function, and relief of suffering, which is often further constricted to relief of symptoms. This is the conceptual box within which we teach medical and nursing students to think; it is a problem-based model.

People come to doctors with "problems." The first thing medical students are taught when they see a new patient is to create a "problem list." It's like the "table of contents" on the medical record. Under each problem on the list, we now teach medical and nursing students to "S.O.A.P. our notes"—to create a *subjective* line item of information from the interview, an *objective* section from our examination and all of the tests that we order, an *assessment* of each of the problems, and then a *plan* of action. Woe to the medical student, intern, or resident who orders a test that doesn't directly relate to a problem on the list or, heaven forbid, who begins an intervention with an ill person that doesn't relate to a problem on that list!

This problem-oriented approach to medicine is a wonderful tool. It was created by Dr. Larry Weed,[1] a professor from the University of Vermont, who probably should have won a Nobel Prize for it. He created the Problem-Oriented Medical Record (POMR) as a way to bring order to medical communications. It revolutionized the way that medical charts are organized and, frankly, the way care plans are developed. For the first time, you could understand and follow another clinician's train of thought, what another had planned, and build on it in some rational way. If you look at medical records prior to the 1970s, when the POMR came into use, they are often chaotic and difficult to follow.

Unfortunately, there have been unintended consequences. The Problem-Oriented Medical Record has become far more than a charting system to become the *de facto* approach for therapeutics in approaching patients and their families, including those facing the end of life. For all its utility, the problem-oriented approach, like all conceptual frameworks, is just a tool, and it has its own limitations.

The experience of dying is more than a set of medical problems to be confronted. In fact, the fundamental nature of dying is not medical at all; it is personal and experiential. Dying is a personal experience. And those of us who do hospice and palliative care know that there is something about the personal experience of patients and families that doesn't fit within the problem-based, problem-bound model of medicine. In fact, it is what gets us up in the morning. Few people working in this field get up in the morning with the sense of, "Oh, boy, I get to treat somebody's pain today. I get to disimpact somebody today!" No, we deal with pain in the bowels because it's important and critically important, but mostly because in doing so, we can preserve something about the personal experience of this time of life for patients and families.

Now, when we talk about the goals of palliative care and hospice, we know that alleviation of symptoms and suffering must be our first priorities, because if we don't deal with pain, bowel function, and related basics of human caring, we won't be able to go beyond that. But as people who are interested in caring through the end of life, we need to talk about what lies beyond symptoms and suffering.

DR. EDWARD W. BASTIAN Tina, though you are not a doctor, your work with cancer patients is often done in the hospital context, and you must deal with that system a great deal; do you have a perspective on this issue?

TINA L. STALEY I don't think there is any point in denying that there is a problem with the health-care system, but I also think we have to be a little more discerning about our stereotype of medical professionals as being "uncaring" or "unfeeling." As someone who works with these people every day, I think that this generalization heaps an unfair judgment on a whole group of individuals who have dedicated their lives to caring for others. Critics will always find it easy to sit on the outside and condemn them, but if they could put themselves in a doctor's shoes, even for a few days, they would gain a new appreciation of their stresses and pressures, and even for their positive motivations.

Doctors go to work every day to deal with pain, with the unknown, with the patient's fear . . . enduring long hours and personal sacrifices of family time. The intentions are generally good—wanting to treat sickness or find a cure is not such a bad intention. But in order to do their job well, they sometimes have to be hyperfocused. We are all organized differently; we all make contributions in different ways. When you approach these health-care professionals with love, not condemnation, you can see transformation. These thoughts are creating a separation between X and Y; we also need to change the "us versus them" consciousness we have, and move on toward a single "us" mentality. This is a part of the change in health care we must focus on. Treating the whole person cannot happen without including the doctors and other health professionals who dedicate their lives to providing the medical component of healing.

DR. EDWARD W. BASTIAN That's a good point. However, just now, as Ira was saying "we need to talk about what lies beyond symptoms and suffering," it occurred to me that some people, including some in the medical field, might ask, "Why? Why do we need to go beyond the alleviation of symptoms and suffering? Won't all be well at that point and our duty discharged, as it were?"

DR. IRA BYOCK Alleviation of symptoms and suffering may be our "first priorities," but they are not our ultimate goals. This is where things get interesting, because I want to say something about the nature of opportunity at the end of life and the positive experience that is possible with the experience of dying. It's not a figment of some novelists' or poets' imaginations. Understanding the nature of opportunity within the range of personal experience of illness and dying is essential to the practice of hospice and palliative care.

DR. EDWARD W. BASTIAN How do we begin to expand the medical model, the mainstream medical model, to accommodate this range of human experience?

DR. IRA BYOCK Well, we already have a good start on it. There is a "treat, prevent, promote" intervention strategy that came from the National Hospice and Palliative Care Organization's Standards

Committee several years ago. It was adopted as a way of framing the discipline's psychosocial and spiritual interventions with people. We *treat* problems that people present us with or we uncover in our routine screening. We *prevent* foreseeable problems that we know are an inherent risk during this turbulent stage in human life. And we *promote* opportunities within the personal realm for people to grow, individually and together.

If this schema sounds familiar, it's actually a conceptual framework for a mainstream branch of medicine. It's called pediatrics! Indeed, while the problem-based model of medicine is mostly an adult internal medicine model, in pediatrics, we were all taught that we must think about the neonate. We must, of course, first *treat* the problems, particularly life-threatening problems that we uncover in the delivery room or in the first few days of life, which we do thorough screening—you know, we calculate APGAR scores,[2] count umbilical cord vessels, check for "hip clicks" and the like, to quickly treat any problem and prevent future problems. Similarly, we watch carefully for conditions like neonatal jaundice and feeding or elimination problems. Beyond treatment and prevention, we *promote* opportunities for each little being to grow individually—to be all he or she can be—for each family to grow together. In pediatrics, it's negligent to do less.

Let me explain. Clinicians and child-care programs didn't always do this. In the 1930s and '40s, in this country, there was an endemic of what came to be known as "pediatric failure to thrive" syndrome. At the time it was called "hospitalism."[3] It occurred sporadically in the community, but was endemic in the foundling homes, the orphanages mostly run by religious orders. In general the care seemed superb—children were perfectly fed, perfectly cleansed, and then swaddled and laid in their bassinette until it was time again for them to be fed, unless they were wet and needed to be changed—and yet, the children "failed to thrive."

René Spitz,[4] a visionary psychiatrist in Denver who looked at the etiology of pediatric failure to thrive, determined that it was caused by a lack of human touch. In the medical papers that Spitz and his group published in the late 1940s, there are poignant descriptions of physical depressions in the bassinettes of the nursery where children had laid for seven months just staring up at the ceiling!

Now, just to give you a sense of the tragic consequences of this "failure of human touch," by the age of five, many of the children in these orphanages had died, mostly from infectious diseases. Among the survivors, 100 percent were mentally retarded.

We know for certain that the problem was a failure of human touch, because once practices were changed, the developmental syndrome was prevented in American orphanages and has largely been relegated to history. But today, tragically, society and clinical professionals are repeating the same mistakes, only in another phase of the life cycle. Today, we are dealing with an endemic geriatric failure to thrive syndrome in many of our nation's nursing homes. The etiology is exactly the same. It is a failure of human touch!

DR. EDWARD W. BASTIAN We have come to see ourselves as demoralized by death, but the truth is that we have demoralized one another in the dying process. Joan, you have made us familiar with the story of your grandmother's lingering death; what was the "better way" for your grandmother? An option better than assisted suicide or a lingering dying?

JOAN HALIFAX ROSHI I could never have "helped her die," as she asked, but there would have been no nursing home for her—no, thank you. Knowing what I know now, it would have been a privilege to *serve* my grandmother through the dying process. I did that for my father, and I feel grateful to have had that opportunity. It would have been great for my parents to do that for my grandmother. But that's not how it went. Nevertheless, her death stirred up a lot for me.

DR. EDWARD W. BASTIAN Ira talked about how doctors involved in palliative care are beginning to approach the dying process; can you tell us how you approach your work with the dying?

JOAN HALIFAX ROSHI I like the guidelines of the American Geriatric Society on how you and I should be cared for: alleviate physical and emotional symptoms; support the autonomy of the patient; work on advance planning that reflects the patient's desires, guarding against inappropriate aggressive interventions; make the end of life precious to the patient and family; ensure that the quality of the patient's life is good despite declining health; minimize the financial burden on the family (and very important, educate the patient in the length of time that insurance companies are actually able to cover treatment); and then there is helping with bereavement.

Apart from these, there are three areas in spiritual care of the dying that seem very important to me. As a spiritual teacher, one is pretty obvious, *the spiritual aspect,* having to do with worldview: what kind of worldview do I have, do you have? They're probably different in relation to deep existential questions. And based on that worldview, what kind of spiritual practices, prayers, songs, and so on, are appropriate to this individual? And then, how do we actualize this in our work? *(See Part II: Resources for Living Fully and Dying Well on pages 149–243.)*

The second area is *community development*. I remember a physician at one of our programs who announced proudly, "I practice patient-centered care." Now, there is nothing wrong with patient-centered care, but about halfway through the training, he says, "You know, I was staying and working with this man, spending hours with him every day because *I had changed my whole practice*—but his wife grew to hate me." He had gotten in the way; he had forgotten that he was just one small part of a community of people who *cared* for the patient.

So the Pew-Fetzer Task Force [5] developed Relationship-Centered Care, recognizing the need to see that the patient is part of a greater network of individuals for whom this matters. And Pew-Fetzer still sees the practitioner, that is, the health-care professional, as a key entity in their paradigm. It is practitioner-patient, practitioner-practitioner, practitioner-community. Yet the web of relationships also includes the patient-community—especially the community of peers who are all suffering from the same kind of illness, providing support and learning in relation to each other. But there's also the postman who's been delivering the mail for thirty-five years, who knows everything about "Miss Lottie, who's dying up there on the second floor." He counts as community too. And so does the family pet. Our vision of community and this vision of relationship-centered care is something that I feel is essential in our care of dying people.

And the third area is *care of the caregiver*—the physical, emotional, mental, spiritual, and social care that's needed to keep a caregiver really deep and on point. How do caregivers care for themselves, keeping themselves strong and resilient, compassionate, and present for those who are dying and grieving? It requires that we actually value the caregiver's well-being. We have to work with secondary trauma and compassion fatigue.

Among professional caregivers, physicians and nurses are rewarded for working overtime, for actually stretching themselves to their very limits and going over to the point where they become numb. They become insensitive not only to the patient, but also to their own situation in a very fundamental way. So valuation of the caregiver's well-being, as Tina pointed out, is something that is very important in our work. If you ask nurses and physicians over the past fifteen years, "Did you have any kind of training in self-care?", the answer is uniformly "no." It's coming now, but slowly. The great paucity of nurses today, the burnout, the addiction problems, the disproportionately high divorce and suicide rate among doctors is a big wake-up call. Caregivers need to care for themselves as well.

TINA L. STALEY As a clinician, I feel that I am always in two worlds. When I sit with a patient, it is so clear that I am dealing both with the consciousness of a patient and yet also with an intensely personal and mysterious inner world. You have to be able to join with the patient in both of these worlds. But it's not only the client that you want to be like that with—you also want to live your life like that.

In more traditional cultures, for example, over morning coffee, with men or women, you'll say, "I had this dream last night," and the next moment, "How are the fields today?" and there's a merging of the two worlds. "Is the business doing well?" is said right next to "I had this feeling. . . ." One goes in and out between inner and outer worlds, between "realities." There is no stark separation. It all just *is*. To help patients, we need to be with them in both inner and outer worlds, and to guide them toward a balance in their own life between the inner and outer realms, to help blend them more harmoniously. Once they get more comfortable with, and less frightened of, the inner, the death process becomes easier. They are not so terrified of being with themselves, so alone with themselves. In death, we cross over from locating our beingness in the outer world to existing entirely in the unseen, inner world. The more practice we have with navigating between the two, the more easily we can make this crossing. In India, they are not so frightened of death.

DR. EDWARD W. BASTIAN What do you mean by "terrified of being with themselves"?

TINA L. STALEY Let me get at this by way of a little detour.

When people are afraid, frustrated, upset, or confused—I find that this consternation is actually a call to love. In our society, we feel that by having compassion and by giving to others, we will reach a loving state of being. But loving and serving others is really only half of the equation. We can get love from others too—in fact, we might have plenty of people showering love on us—but in order for love to truly change us, to be transformational, it must come from within ourselves.

I once had a forty-nine-year-old patient named Lisa who was a "supermom" and who also ran a successful company. She never slowed down; she hardly ever even sat down. One day I asked her, "What would you do for your husband if he were sick?" She said, "I would have him go to bed; I would make him soup; I'd rub his head." I asked, "What about your daughter?" and she gave the same answers. But when I asked, "What about you?" she said, "I'd tell myself to 'Get out of bed,' and ask, 'Why are you lying there?'" So I asked her, "Why can't you express the same love and the same care for yourself as you do for your family?" With tears in her eyes, she admitted, "Because I've never heard those words before." "Are you open to teaching yourself those words?" I nudged. And she was. For the next two months, every night before she went to bed, she wrote, "I love you," twenty times, and she listed the things that she loved about herself. I suggested that she talk to herself the same way she would have loved to hear her mom talk to her. I "prescribed" that she brush her own hair, take a bath, and sit for a few quiet moments in front of the fire every night before she went to bed. It was hard for her at first, but she worked on these assignments, and over time she blossomed. She was beginning to love herself.

I often ask my patients, "If you were to die, would you want to take yourself with you? If not, why not? What would you like to change so that you would like yourself to go with you on this journey?" Some people say "yes," some are taken aback by the question, and a lot say "no." They don't feel worthy, even of their own company! Cancer patients can have a tremendous amount of guilt and shame; they may have trouble feeling that they deserve the best that life has to offer. They absolutely must work through this layer of guilt and shame before they can feel self-love.

Lisa was pretty typical in this respect. She was ashamed of being a burden to others. She felt guilty of not having given enough, not having been a good enough person, not having lived up to her own, or others', expectations of her. Like many people, she was doubting whether she really deserved to live.

With these serious questions about their own self-worth, people enact, in a sense, their own Judgment Day. It can be excruciating. Forgiveness—of themselves, as well as others—thus becomes a tremendously important task. *(See Tina Staley's* Forgiveness *in "Visualizations for Emotional Healing" on page 231.)*

When you learn to love life, to forgive and love yourself, it doesn't really matter whether you live or die—because you recognize your true essence, your most precious possession and valued companion. Our self becomes a sort of base, a grounding presence, on the inside. It's always with us. It allows us to feel that whatever happens on the outside we can withstand it; we will be okay. Life will be okay. And so will death.

Because of my experience with numerous breast-cancer patients, I believe it is worth asking, even in this conversation, "Why is it so difficult for women to love themselves in our culture?" There are clearly huge barriers that get in the way and prevent women from cultivating self-love. Not that men are excluded from this, but it is pronounced among the women I have worked with.

Our language reflects this—"selfish" and "self-centered"—these are words with huge negative connotations, making loving ourselves seem like a bad thing. We feel guilty for taking care of ourselves. Some of this, to be sure, is conditioning by our culture. We are praised for looking outward, for setting aside our own desires and needs in favor of helping others. But we were all born with an essence that is good and pure and that we need to fully own, express, celebrate, and love.

I've often wondered how some people can live through the most difficult of situations—concentration camp, rape, deprivation—and still have the capacity to tap into that essence. Fortunately we are not all challenged in these extreme ways, but we do all share the common challenge of dying. And we all must rise to the occasion in this way, at the end of life, somehow, no matter what we did or did not do. Death gives us all the opportunity to find our beautiful, pure, inner nature.

FOUR

Living Through Our Dying

To the inhabitants of New York, Paris, or London, death is a word that is never uttered because it burns the lips. The Mexican, on the other hand, frequents it, mocks it, caresses it, sleeps with it, entertains it; it is one of his favorite playthings and his most enduring love.

OCTAVIO PAZ
The Labyrinth of Solitude

THE EPIPHANY

ONE AFTERNOON IN my room in Woody Creek, Colorado, I had an epiphany. I'd been studying a lot of Eastern philosophy, when all of a sudden something came over me, and I said to myself, "No matter what it takes in my lifetime, I will follow this spiritual journey." And soon after that epiphany, I became intensely interested in death and dying, and read every book that I could get a hold of.

A month later, my brother was diagnosed with leukemia, and I spent the next four months of my life with him in a bone-marrow transplant ward. I was simply there for him. I loved spending time with the people at the hospital, but I was also aware of being immersed in an environment of fear. Cancer is a difficult process for everyone, but especially for those who feel alone. I remember a terror-stricken sixteen-year-old girl sitting by her dying mother's side, and an Hispanic family trying to navigate their way through the health system, to understand what was happening to their loved one, when they couldn't speak the language. The fear was obvious in these cases, but it is no less present in other patients who are caught unprepared to leave life, and uncertain about the unknown that lies so near in their future. My brother did well, and I'm happy to say that he and his family are happy and healthy today, eight years later.

Shortly after his illness, though, I came back to Aspen and shared in the last year of my best friend Jeannie Renchard's life. Jeannie had Stage IV breast cancer, which over time had spread throughout her body, to her bones, her brain, and deep tissues. Jeannie and I spent countless hours talking about the meaning of life, dying, her treatment, and her experiences with cancer. Every day, we discussed how we participated in life in that day.

Even though Jeannie didn't always feel well, we were still able to become girls again, children at play in the world and loving life. We lay under olive trees; we built a clubhouse; we dressed up in costumes; we picked bushels of cherries and ate almost as many on the spot. We pretended we were beauty pageant queens. We listened to opera. One time, we rented a laughing machine and played it for an hour, laughing hysterically along with the canned guffaws. We discussed book after book, poem after poem, song after song—on life, love, passion. Paradoxically, Jeannie's dying made us both so much more alive.

One day, after several cancer-related losses, as I was stepping out of the shower, it suddenly hit me: "Every cancer patient in America should have an advocate. No one should have to go through this process alone." I think I was receiving in that moment the guidance that would become my life mission. And that moment was the beginning of what became the Aspen Cancer Guide Program at Aspen Valley Hospital, in partnership with Aspen Center for Integral Health, and what has now evolved into a national program called Pathfinders.

TINA STALEY

I n the pages that follow, Dr. Edward W. Bastian talks with Dr. Ira Byock and Tina L. Staley about the process of continuing to "live" even as we are dying. Dr. Ira Byock, whom we met in the previous chapter, is the author of *Dying Well: Peace and Possibilities at the End of Life*. Tina L. Staley, to whom we were also introduced in the last chapter, is the founder of Pathfinders, an integrative, whole-person approach to cancer care addressing the mind, body, and spiritual needs of each individual cancer patient while working side by side with the medical team. In this chapter, they tackle the question: How can we assess and enhance quality of life for the person who is dying? — *Ed.*

DR. EDWARD W. BASTIAN Earlier, Reb Zalman talked about Elisabeth Kübler-Ross's patient who said, "I want to live through my dying." What does that mean to you, Dr. Byock?

DR. IRA BYOCK One of my mentors, Dr. Balfour Mount,[1] and his colleague Dr. John Scott[2] published an article in the *Journal of Chronic Disease* in 1983, talking about how you measure "quality of life" in somebody at the end of their life. There they talked about a young patient named "Eric," who in dying, commented that his final months, which had been characterized by relentless physical deterioration and considerable suffering, had been "the best of my life." Then they pointed out that on the day he made that comment, "this young athlete, scholar and executive, who had measured ten out of ten on the Spitzer Quality of Life Index[3] throughout his life, measured just two out of ten." So clearly Eric was referring to something not embraced by the scales measuring activities of daily living and not reflected in the Spitzer Quality of Life Index.

If you look at the quality-of-life indices that are often being used in health care today, you'll see embedded within them an assumption that as a person's functional status declines, their quality of life declines. Usually, that assumption is tagged to their independence. When a person can no longer drive, their quality of life is assumed to drop. When they can no longer walk stairs or help around the house or, heaven forbid, toilet themselves, their quality of life is assumed to be poor. Thus, when we aggregate quality-of-life scores, we find out that when people are dying, their quality of life is terrible — *unless you ask them.*

So years ago, in an attempt to bridge this gap, I wrote a quality-of-life tool in collaboration with Melanie Merriman[4] called the Missoula-Vitas Quality of Life Index[5] or MVQoLI for short. It has five dimensions, which are all entirely subjective. The Missoula-Vitas doesn't obviate symptom frequency and intensity scales or objective functional assessment scales; it simply complements them with a subjective perspective.

The last two dimensions of the tool, the intrapersonal domain and the transcendent or transpersonal domain, can give you a sense that even these realms of human experience can be assessed and measured. The intrapersonal, which I also call the well-being dimension of the tool, is a self-assessment of a person's internal condition—a subjective sense of wellness or *dis-ease,* along with a sense of either contentment or lack of contentment.

One of the items in the intrapersonal dimension presents two choices (in a double-item format) and asks the person to mark closest to the statement with which he or she agrees: "My affairs are in order; I could die today with a clear mind" on the left, and "My affairs are not in order; I am worried that many things are left unresolved" on the right.

Then the Missoula-Vitas asks, in a single-item format with choices being "disagree" on the left and "agree" on the right, "I am more satisfied with myself as a person now than I was before my illness."

DR. EDWARD W. BASTIAN And what kind of responses do you get? It is hard to imagine a favorable response in those circumstances.

DR. IRA BYOCK I still use this tool in practice, and it often elicits very useful responses. And not uncommonly, we get to this item and people say to me, "Really? People say that—that they are more satisfied with themselves now?" So it's interesting that the assessment tool *itself* opens up the possibility in people's minds that there might be something of value still ahead.

Then we come to the transcendent or transpersonal dimension of the tool, measuring the degree to which a person experiences a sense of connection with an enduring construct and the sense of meaning and purpose in life. A few of the questions are these, in contrasting-statement format: "I have a better sense of meaning in my life now than I have had in the past" on the left, and "I have less of a sense of meaning in my life now than I have had in the past," on the right. Another is "Life has become more precious to me; every day is a gift," on the left, and "Life has lost all value for me; every day is a burden," on the right

The tool gives clinicians and teams a better sense of where to direct psychosocial or spiritual interventions, or at least where to further explore through interviews with a person potential sources of distress and well-being.

DR. EDWARD W. BASTIAN So it is important not to make assumptions about quality of life for dying people, nor to project our own judgments onto them?

TINA L. STALEY I think we tend to assume that the nearness of death itself diminishes someone's quality of life. And so, to protect them—or maybe just to shield ourselves—we tiptoe around the issue. The very fact of death, of an end to our time in this life, makes many of us very uncomfortable. We go to great lengths to avoid or sidestep it. Then, because we don't talk about death, especially not with the one who is dying, death becomes, as you mentioned earlier, the proverbial elephant in the room. Everybody sees it, everybody navigates around it, but nobody mentions it. Many patients come to me with a great hunger to talk about their own death as a result of this avoidance.

One patient, Catherine, even pleaded with me, "*Please* talk to me about dying." She said, "My friends won't talk about it. My husband won't talk about it. My medical team won't even talk about it. What I want for our session is to talk about dying." She described herself as a "realist." Her breast cancer had metastasized throughout her body, and she knew she was going to die from it. But she couldn't get anyone else to accept this reality. "I feel like I'm screaming inside, and no one wants to hear me."

One of the processes we use with people who are dying — and you'll hear about this from others — is the Life Review. In a Life Review, we guide a person along an introspective journey back through his or her life, looking at all of the main events and people. In reexamining relationships, places, times, and tasks, we are in essence helping the person write the last chapter of his or her life. We would never write a book and stop before crafting the last chapter. Why, then, do we ignore this most critical and powerful "chapter" when writing the story of our own life? From the Life Review, we also end up with some tangibles that are incredibly meaningful for both the dying person and loved ones — a workbook, mementos, a treasure box of significant items, such as poems and personal belongings. *(See Zalman Schachter-Shalomi's "Life Review Exercises" on pages 153–160.)*

For Catherine's Life Review, I asked her to find one friend who would be willing to join her in our discussion, to share the experience of talking about dying. Together, the three of us talked about Life Review questions that are valuable to everyone going through the dying process: "Do you want to die alone? Or do you want to die with someone else present? Who would that be? If you could plan a perfect last day, what would it be — what would you eat; where would you be; who would be with you; what music would you listen to? Is there anyone you would like to have a caring conversation with? Who? Is there anyone whose forgiveness you would want to ask? Who would you like to forgive?" *(See Zalman Schachter-Shalomi's "Exercises for Facing Our Mortality" on pages 161–169 and "Exercises for Healing Emotional Wounds and Forgiveness" on pages 171–177.)*

Catherine and her friend, Mary, both walked through this process, and in the exchange, they decided that Mary would shoot a video of Catherine for her sixteen-year-old son. Catherine also wanted her unborn grandchildren to know who she was, to have this gift from her. She spun out her stories, passing them down to next generations: her first sight of her son's father, her husband's days as a hippy, her wishes for her son, her own wedding, and who she hopes for him to marry. Mary, an amateur photographer, took the film in three settings: the trail behind Catherine's house, her back porch, and the Duke Garden, a lovely botanical garden setting always bedecked with flowers. The two friends' relationship has itself blossomed into a whole new level of truth, a new depth of communication, through this process. Both women have become more alive, more *consciously* alive. The Life Review gave them an opportunity to value the time that they had together and to cherish every moment that they still have. And their process opened the door for others to join Catherine on her end-of-life journey.

As of this time, her husband, her doctor, and several friends have all let down their initial defenses and supported her in exploring her life and her death. Even her doctor has had heart-opening discussions with Catherine about death.

DR. EDWARD W. BASTIAN What do you think is at the root of our avoidance of death?

TINA L. STALEY I believe that it's fear. Jerry Jampolsky,[6] who founded the Center for Attitudinal Healing, taught me that we either live in a "state of love" or we live in a "state of fear." And fear can encompass many things — anger, jealousy, resentment — so I have always been curious: How can you take those types of feelings (while dealing with cancer) and turn them into something profound, something positive? What is the alchemy that allows someone who is in a metaphorical desert to turn around and see a flower?

DR. EDWARD W. BASTIAN You work directly with people living with and often dying from cancer every day; have you ever seen someone "living through their dying" as Elisabeth Kübler-Ross's patient wished to do?

TINA L. STALEY Though I don't often explain it this way, the simple underlying purpose of Pathfinders[7] — and really, the mission for all of us working with people at the end of life — is to help people move from a place of fear to a place of understanding, acceptance, and love. We teach coping skills, help patients rediscover their inner strengths, and create self-care plans and support systems. This all leads to personal recovery and love, and it is only in love that we have peace of mind. The minute people are diagnosed with cancer, they feel as if they are caught beneath a wave, as a colleague of mine [Dr. Keith Block][8] described it. Terror washes over them, leaving them disoriented and unable to think clearly. In Pathfinders, we work through that terror-stricken, overwhelmed stage; we get to the basic fear of dying, and hopefully, after a lot of personal recovery, we arrive at a place of love and acceptance.

One patient of mine who clearly "lived through his dying" was Tim. He had been diagnosed with leukemia and was simply terrified. Tim was an active, outdoorsy, athletic man in his mid-forties. He was single and loved spending time with his dog and was absolutely amazing with children; kids adored him, and he loved them. He was, you could say, a youthful soul bursting with life. But he got terminal cancer.

On his first few visits, he came into my office sweating and shaking. "I'm so scared to die!" he told me. His chemotherapy was failing him, and he was being sent away for a bone-marrow transplant. As it turned out, he didn't qualify for the transplant, so he returned to Aspen with a grim prognosis. After this roller coaster of failed cure-seeking, he came back to me, saying, "I know it's going to happen. Will you help me die?" And I said, "Not only will I help you die; I will help you *to die well*. You will not be in pain, and you will not be alone."

Over time, Tim began to relax. We worked on what was unresolved in his life; we looked at the joyful and the sad moments; we spoke about where his life had meaning and where he had made contributions; we talked about who would take care of his dog; we even planned his funeral. And through this whole process, by actually befriending the "elephant in the room," he let go of his fear and was able to talk about his death. He underwent a whole spectrum of mind-body care—visualization, breath work, massage, acupuncture, and relaxation practices—that helped ease his anxiety and bring him to a state of peace.

Eventually, Tim went into a coma-like state about a week-and-a-half before his passing. We all thought it would be a matter of days. Then, all of a sudden, unbelievably, he woke up from his coma in the most peaceful, joyful state. He went to the ski company and said good-bye to all of his friends. He went to the rafting company and took leave of his friends there. It was Sunday, and he said to me, "Tina, I think I'm going to *'go'* on Tuesday. I'm ready." Monday morning, he said, "It might be Wednesday; I got a good night's sleep." There were people he still wanted to see. Doesn't this show how much control an individual can have at the end of life?

We don't see this often, but those of us who work in the end-of-life field find that there is some degree of control and some organizing plan at the end of a person's life. Who is there, who the dying person chooses to have in the room with them, may appear to be coincidental, but it seems to play out as if it were the patient's choice. Tim provides a good example.

Over his last weeks, an entourage of past girlfriends, acquaintances, and others who had known and appreciated him came to visit Tim in his home. However, Tuesday was a relatively quiet day. I sent Diane, a "Valley Angel" (a volunteer nurse with the Cancer Guides program), to see him. A friend who had known Tim for over twenty years was with him when Diane arrived. Even though Diane and Tim had never met, Tim spoke with her for four hours about his life. When he had finished, he said, "You know, there is a sense of real relief . . . almost like I have to *'go'* now . . . but I have to pee first." So Diane helped him to the bathroom, and all of a sudden, he died in her arms. It may seem strange to say, but Diane reported, "Off he went in true grace."

That's the privilege of working with someone who really *lives* through their dying. It really is a privilege to do this work. There's lots of light and passion in both living and dying. Our work is actually about *living*. It's all a continuum—passion and dying, passion and living—and we try to help people live their lives to the fullest, every moment right through their last breath.

DR. IRA BYOCK I'm glad that Tina brought up the phrase "dying well." Notice that in the phrase the word "well" is commonly assumed to be an adverb that modifies the experience of dying. But you can also hear it as an adjective that describes the person who is dying. Can a person be "well" during the time that he or she is dying? If not, are we saying that in our dying we all must be pathologic simply because we're mortal? I think Tina's case study of Tim demonstrates that a person can be "well" while dying.

Think about an individual who you know, who in your own assessment is among the most emotionally and spiritually adept and robust people you've met; knowing that he or she too will eventually die, must that person be considered "unwell" during this time of life? Can people be "well" during the time that they're dying? And can people become *more* "well" during this time?

How we care for one another, how we care for the most ill, advanced elderly, infirm among us is, I believe, the central challenge, not only facing our professions, but also facing our generation. It is a key criterion on which historians of the future will judge the moral worth of our generation.

The good news is that we can meet that challenge, but it will require a commitment of energy, professionalism, and creativity that is almost unprecedented. I believe that what we're doing now, talking about the full dimensions of hospice and palliative care, human caring through the end of life, represents a shift that needs to occur in our society and culture's approach to the end of life. It is a shift from seeing dying solely as a time of misery and suffering, a shift toward understanding that dying is a part of full and even healthy living, and a time of remarkable opportunity.

Simply by doing what we do best, caring for the people we meet, by doing it within a team of caring providers, by keeping our commitment and that of our team's strong, by education and preparation, and by acknowledging not only the capacity for suffering we all have, but also the lifelong capacity for human development that we all have, we have an opportunity to contribute to a healthy reincorporation of the value of this time we call "dying" within the ongoing mystery of human life. That is our great opportunity.

FIVE

The Great Opportunity

Death is our first completely personal act and therefore, by reason of its very being, the place above all others for the awakening of consciousness, for freedom, for the encounter with God, for the final decision about eternal destiny.

LADISLAUS BOROS
The Mystery of Death

DYING WELL

PEOPLE SOMETIMES ASK me, "How did you get into this field?" Well, it happened back in 1978 in a boat-gray county teaching hospital in Fresno, California. I got into this field because in dealing with symptoms and suffering of dying patients, every once in a while something remarkable and seemingly unexplainable happened. I'd meet a patient who described him- or herself as "well." I remember a man

I'll call "Mr. Rodriquez." He had cancer and knew he was dying. He was aware that he would not get out of the hospital alive. I once spoke with him on my rounds, inquiring about his pain and basic medical issues, and I asked him, "Mr. Rodriquez, how are you today?" He looked me right in the face and said, "I'm well, doctor. How are you?"

Now, in all honesty, I heard that a few times before I got it. At first, I heard it and said, "Oh, it's the morphine; he's euphoric." "Oh, it's the steroids; he's got a touch of mania." But I realized after a while—the third or fourth time I had an experience like that—that dismissing such comments was disrespectful, that the universe was trying to teach me something, and if I was simply humble enough to listen, maybe I would learn something—how a person can be "well" during the experience of dying.

DR. IRA BYOCK

In the pages that follow, Dr. Edward W. Bastian talks with Dr. Ira Byock, Tina L. Staley, and Joan Halifax Roshi about the unique opportunities that are afforded us in the dying process: Dr. Ira Byock introduces some of the themes covered in his book, *The Four Things That Matter Most: A Book about Living*; Tina L. Staley, a licensed clinical social worker, talks about the accumulated "baggage" of life that we bring into the dying process; and Joan Halifax Roshi, abbot and founder of the Upaya Zen Center in Santa Fe, New Mexico, discusses Buddhist approaches to dying. —*Ed.*

DR. EDWARD W. BASTIAN So how do we take advantage of that "opportunity" that death and dying afford us?

DR. IRA BYOCK At the very least, knowledge that death is approaching provides an opportunity to do the Life Review Tina talked about before: to share feelings; to complete business and personal affairs; to complete relationships, to leave nothing left unsaid; to resolve previously strained relationships, perhaps between a father and son who haven't spoken in years, or previous spouses after a bitter divorce, or a brother or sister long estranged; a chance to grieve together, acknowledging the loss to both parties; a chance to explore realms of meaning and purpose, realms of connection to something larger than ourselves that are indeed part and parcel of the human experience of life's end.

DR. EDWARD W. BASTIAN What are some of the steps you take people through in this process?

DR. IRA BYOCK If we conceptualize each individual person as a set of concentric spheres comprising our personhood, we can make a fairly simple plan for life completion.

On the outside, we can begin with completing our fiscal and business affairs, our legal affairs: such as transferring the deed on the car and the house, the bank accounts, and the like. Next, we can look at our relationships with our nonintimate, casual acquaintances, co-workers or congregants in our faith community, the dry cleaner and the fellow who makes us lattes in the morning every day. That involves saying the things that would be left unsaid, expressing appreciation and, when necessary, "taking leave."

Going a little deeper has to do with achieving a sense of meaning about our individual life. That involves the task-work of Life Review and the telling of one's stories. The practice of Life Review is a nonthreatening way for people to get a sense about the meaning of their own life. Myrna Lewis and Robert Butler talk about Life Review as "an opportunity to reexamine the whole of one's life and to make sense of it, both on its own terms and in comparison to the lives of others. Identity may be reexamined and restructured. There's a chance to resolve old problems, to make amends and to restore harmony with friends and relatives." So *storytelling can be therapeutic. (See Zalman Schachter-Shalomi's "Life Review Exercises" on pages 153–160.)*

Deeper still is the experience of loving oneself (as we saw in Tina's example about Lisa in Chapter 3), an important developmental landmark. The task-work here involves self-acknowledgment and self-forgiveness. The human condition is an imperfect condition, and we will die imperfect. My advice to people is, "Get over it!" I mean, thankfully, we are not called to be perfect. We are just human, and that's good enough. But we are often raised as more of human *doings* than human *beings*.

For instance, I'm an adult child of Jewish parents. I'm sure that is in the *DSM-IV*,[1] right next to the Adult Children of Catholic Parents! It's a condition with no known cure, which is to say, we grow up in a world of expectations. Sometimes, I sit with people and ask them to take in some deep breaths so that I can teach them a relaxation technique. I say, "Envision a big wheel, and on the outskirts of the wheel is a sentence, 'I am not a bad person; I am not a bad person.'" Can you say that?" Often, people look down and say "no." *(See Zalman Schachter-Shalomi's "Exercises for Healing Emotional Wounds and Forgiveness" on pages 171–177 and*

Joan Halifax's Affirmations for Forgiveness *in "Practices for Transforming Pain and Suffering" on page 185.)*

Why? What could be so wrong with them? Once it was a cancer patient who smoked, and I said, "Oh, it's the smoking, isn't it?" I'm all for smoking cessation, but you've got to know that these days, people come to the end of life, not uncommonly, feeling they inflicted themselves with the mortality gene by smoking. So I gently, lovingly challenge it. I said to him, "You know, I care for people all the time. I care for a lot of people who have never smoked and are still dying. My goal is for you to be able to look in the mirror, right smack in the mirror, and say, 'Boy, I'd like a cigarette! But I'm still a good person.' Because, you are!"

And notice, even though I do this in a lighthearted fashion, we're doing profound clinical work.

DR. EDWARD W. BASTIAN I just want to stop you for a moment. You are using the language of moving through layers to a core . . . so, I am wondering if this is necessarily sequential work?

DR. IRA BYOCK Human development at the end of life is not sequential. Human beings, certainly adults, have worked on various parts of themselves, and that pretty much endures. But "loving oneself" really has to precede the next layer and developmental landmark, that of "the experienced love of others," because other people can love you, and if you don't feel worthy, you simply can't feel it. You make up excuses, "Well, if they really knew who I was, they wouldn't love me." So it's as if it goes right past you. And that sense of acceptance, that sense of feeling other people's love is an important part of human development through the end of life.

Then we can move on to a sense of completion with our intimate relationships, our family and friends, people we love, or once loved, and that involves saying the things that would be left unsaid and saying good-bye. Through all of this work, I have learned that before any significant relationship is complete, people have to have said at least four things before good-bye: "Please forgive me"; "I forgive you"; "Thank you"; and "I love you."

Deeper still is acceptance of the *finale* of life, one's existence as an individual. Now, notice I'm down into deeply spiritual realms. I'm not changing the experience. The experience is *as it is.* I'm just applying a developmental framework to what is the continuum of human experience. This involves task-work like the acknowledgment of the totality of personal expression of the depth of the tragedy of our impending death, our emotional withdrawal from worldly affairs, and an emotional connection to an enduring construct, an acceptance of dependency.

Now we realize that dependency is clearly a stressor that contributes to people suffering. But it is also a fact that in the human condition, many of us will be physically dependent during the end of our life, much as we were as infants and toddlers. That too is part of the human experience. It is not an assault on our dignity; it is part of being human. This is where Ram Dass,[2] in his teachings, and Stephen Levine,[3] in his book *Who Dies?,* say, "Isn't it interesting that I'm no longer the breadwinner of the family, coach of the kid's soccer team . . . and yet, today was such a good day. Who am I now?" *(See Zalman Schachter-Shalomi's "Exercises for Facing Our Mortality" on pages 161–169.)*

So, lastly, from a developmental perspective, we have a surrender to the transcendent, that ultimate letting go. Here the task-work and the person are so entwined that that last volitional act defines this landmark. As things fall away, as the stuff that fills our Palm Pilots and our day planners becomes less relevant to our life situation, it is normal for people to begin asking, "Well, what is life about anyway? What's my life about? Where am I going next? What is life in the universe really about?"

DR. EDWARD W. BASTIAN Tina, do you find that you need to take people through a similar process?

TINA L. STALEY Unfortunately, yes; many of us die and come into our dying process carrying a lot of baggage. Self-deprecation is one of the most common burdens people take with them right up to the end of life.

Why do so many of us judge ourselves and put ourselves down? It seems to be a particularly American issue; other cultures don't seem to do this as much. In my travels, I've seen village after village where babies are passed around from adult to adult, children run in and out of each others' huts, the adults share in chores and in fun. In these contexts, a focus of disliking oneself seems absurd. Everyone is so connected; the notion of individuality doesn't hold sway, and the tendency to dwell on one's own shortcomings just simply disappears.

In our culture, I suspect self-loathing starts with a deep-seated sense of separation, of being an individual who is separate and apart from others around us. From this vantage point, we compare ourselves to others. It's natural; if you observe your thoughts over the course of a day, you'll see judgments cropping up all the time. And through this habit of comparison and judgment—whether it's in sports, grades, work, or our looks—we are continually defining ourselves as either one-up (a vulnerable position) or one-down (a not-good-enough position). Either position leads to a sense of unworthiness—of personal failing—built upon our separation from one another.

I think at the time of death, it's this sense of separation that causes pain. Imagine how lonely the experience of death would be if you truly felt like you had to face it all by yourself. This is why people are so grateful for phone calls, visits, or notes at the end of life. These little gestures make them feel connected to their own kind and make the thought of dying easier. For, ultimately, we judge ourselves by how well we connected with others, asking, "Did I love well enough?" or "Was I loved?"

And so in my work with people, and in my efforts to help them learn self-love, I look for some way that they can feel connected. For a lot of people, God, or some sort of Higher Source or Spirit, is this connecting force. But not for everyone. People can find a meaningful sense of connection through nature, a pet, art, or another person.

I once worked with a cancer patient named Jim who was a jazz musician. He lived alone and didn't believe in God. He had centered his whole life around music and derived his purpose and meaning in life from it. Toward the end of his life, Jim became frightened and bitter about dying. I sat with him at one point when he was too upset and angry to talk. Instead, for half an hour, we listened to his music. Soulful strains of jazz and blues flowed around us. After a while, his tension released its grip, and we discussed how music enabled him to feel, to connect with something larger than himself, and to be inside himself in a peaceful, meditative way.

Jim's cancer progressed rapidly, and as he was dying, I put on his music, and he literally died tapping out the beats with his fingers! His connection to music carried him right through his death and onward to the next level. For Jim, it didn't matter whether any higher power, God, was in the music. What mattered was that he found a path to peace through connection.

For some people, like Jim, connection happens slowly and progressively, over time. For others, it can happen in a moment. Stan, a sixty-two-year-old patient, achieved a reputation in the cancer center where I worked for being not only excessively pessimistic, but also hostile and resistant to support. He met with me only because his doctor insisted and seemed determined not to let me get near him emotionally. If I said "sun," he said "rain." When I asked him about "God," he retorted, "I'm an atheist." Nothing could reach him. Partway through his chemotherapy, he came into the hospital for another treatment session. It was fall foliage season in Colorado, and the trees were all ablaze in reds and oranges. Stan's treatment ended early that day, but he didn't want to spend the extra time talking with me. I suggested instead that he go to The Bells, a beautiful scenic mountain overlook not far from the clinic. To my surprise, he took my suggestion and drove there. Two hours later, he returned and had the nurse on the floor call me out of an appointment. The nurse and I immediately guessed that he had encountered some crisis. I quickly sought him out in the waiting room and found him crying. "Tina," he said, "I had no idea that life could be so beautiful."

Stan had seen, *really seen*, the full magnificence of the mountain covered in brilliant colors. At that moment, he connected—maybe for the first time—with Beauty. He died two weeks later, changed from this awareness of the mystery of awe and wonder.

DR. EDWARD W. BASTIAN In a way, that brings us right up to the door of spirituality. What does spirituality have to tell us about death and dying as an "opportunity," Joan?

JOAN HALIFAX ROSHI A 1997 Gallop poll on death and dying said, "The American people want to reclaim and reassert the spiritual dimensions of dying." But "spirituality" is not an institutional matter. It cannot be adjudicated per se. It is a deeply personal matter, and one needs to be very sensitive as a pastoral person that you're not laying a spiritual "trip" on somebody who has a very different perspective. *(See Zalman Schachter-Shalomi's "Exercises for Facing Our Mortality" on pages 161–169.)*

In spiritual exploration, it is very important to explore individually, to explore for ourselves, and to ask: What is our own view of what dying means? Is dying a good thing or a bad thing for us? Is it an opportunity or a defeat? Do we believe that there's an afterlife? If we don't believe that, does that shape our behavior in a way that's positive or problematic? Are we in touch with the truth of impermanence? Or are we fixated by nature, trying to grasp and possess? Ultimately, we are going to be asked to give it all up. So it is very good to see the truth of impermanence, but maybe that is not part of how we see our world. Another issue is: What is our view of pain? Is pain redemptive or a curse? What is our vision of suffering? Is it an opportunity or a defeat? What about the value of altruism from the perspective of caregiving? And what gives our life and our death meaning?

Sir Walter Scott said, "Is death the last sleep? No, it is the last and final awakening."[4] From the Buddhist perspective, death is the greatest opportunity for liberation.

My third Zen teacher, Tetsugen Roshi—Bernie Glassman[5] —works with three tenets that I have found helpful in working with issues of pain, suffering, dying, death, and grieving. The first tenet is "not knowing." Can we simply sit with dying, or a dying person, with a kind of "beginner's mind," just open, instead of always coming at things in a formulaic way? Can we actualize a "tolerance for the inconceivable" as Vimalakirti[6] calls it? A hospice worker once told me, "You know, I drive up to a patient's house. I turn off the car. I sit there for a beat and try to forget everything I know, and then I walk into the patient's home with that kind of openness." We're not talking about being stupid here. There are skills that we have as caregivers that are essential, but this kind of openness, this capacity to accept the unacceptable, to acknowledge that you really "don't know" is also essential.

The second tenet is "bearing witness." Bearing witness is an experience of being present for what is happening, really being present for all of it. And the third tenet Glassman Roshi calls "healing" or "loving action," meaning how we can serve all suffering beings.

DR. EDWARD W. BASTIAN A moment ago, you mentioned "pain" and "suffering." What is the difference between the two in Buddhism?

JOAN HALIFAX ROSHI *Pain* is mental and physical discomfort of varying degrees and *suffering* is the story around the pain. As a Buddhist, I hope to be able to say with discernment, "I am in pain, but I am not suffering." This is a very different perspective than we usually have, and one that can be very beneficial to the one who is in pain. *(See Joan Halifax's "Practices for Transforming Pain and Suffering" on pages 179–186.)*

There are many good practices for working with pain around the experience of dying: relaxation techniques, breath practice, concentration and observation of pain, letting go into the pain, objectifying the pain, moving attention away from the pain, considering others who have pain like we do, living with our pain with great equanimity, and making pain a teaching on impermanence, strength, and compassion.

DR. EDWARD W. BASTIAN Would you say more about some of the practices that support one in the dying process?

JOAN HALIFAX ROSHI Well, first there are the values that support us. Living an ethical and wholesome life supports one in the process. This is really hard if you are suddenly diagnosed with a severe illness. You know you are heading toward active dying, and you have made a whole mess of your life, you have got a long list of debts, so it is a lot to work with. But you can still start to think of others before yourself. Practice generosity. Give away the things that you like, that you are attached to. Death is going to take them anyway. Use hardship to build patience and perspective. Contemplate the truth of your mortality and feel grateful for what you have now. Develop a positive and realistic image of dying. In the Christian tradition, medieval monks used to whisper into one another's ears, "Remember death," as a spiritual practice. In the Buddhist tradition, we work with the interdependence of two components: wisdom and compassion, *strong back, soft front.* One practice teaches us the truth of impermanence; the other practice nurtures equanimity and compassion. *(See Joan Halifax's "Practices for Transforming Pain and Suffering" on pages 179–186 and* Facing Loss *in "Practices for the Caregiver and the Bereaved" on page 225.)*

Some of the Buddhist practices that support the dying process are stabilization and insight practices, practices that are about developing positive qualities, like loving-kindness, compassion, joy, and equanimity. In meditation, we actually guide our thoughts and behaviors according to our attention, producing states of mind that positively affect the immune system, reduce stress, and support a capacity for an individual to bend with life more easily.

The development of enduring attention is very important. We are kind of an ADD[7] culture, but a capacity for staying on point is really necessary in the dying process. Without this basic life skill, a person is going to have a hard time being present to their own dying or for someone else who is dying. So this capacity to practice open presence and enduring attention is very important. At first it takes effort, but after a while, it becomes effortless. *(See Joan Halifax's* Giving and Receiving: A Practice of Mercy *in "Practices for the Caregiver and the Bereaved" on page 209.)*

In Buddhism, we engage in various practices that are conducive to deep compassion and mercy, such as *tonglen*, exchanging self with other, where we really allow ourselves to see through the eyes of the other; to feel the pain and suffering of another and to bring it into our whole body, mind, and heart-field. This kind of practice strengthens our unselfishness and fosters compassion.

More esoteric practices, particularly from Tibetan Buddhism, relate to the bardos, the phases through which we pass in death, states of consciousness; sleep and dream practices; death-point and clear light meditations; and consciousness transference at the time of death, called *powa*. On one of my trips to Mount Kailash, I saw an old man doing powa. Buddhist teacher, Chagdud Tulku Rinpoche,[8] was insistent that his students learn the powa practice.

It is an important practice that you do at the time of the death or to assist someone else in his or her transition between life and death. *(See Joan Halifax's "Meditations and Preparation for the Moment of Death" on pages 187–206.)*

From the Zen Buddhist perspective, of course, it is simply using our daily life as practice—changing a bedpan, and doing it not as something that's aversive, but actually as a mindfulness practice—seeing it all as practice.

SIX

Purgatory and the River of Light and Gaia, Samsara, Narnia

Leaving aside the rational arguments against any certainty in these matters, we must not forget that for most people it means a great deal to assume that their lives will have an indefinite continuity beyond their present existence. They live more sensibly, feel better, and are more at peace. . . . A man should be able to say he has done his best to form a conception of life after death, or to create some image of it—even if he must confess his failure. Not to have done so is a vital loss. For the question that is posed to him is the age-old heritage of humanity: an archetype, rich in secret life, which seeks to add itself to our own individual life in order to make it whole.

CARL JUNG
Memories, Dreams, Reflections

THE COMMUNION OF SAINTS

MY MOTHER DIED on June 1, 1983. On June 1, 1984, I was sitting in our chapel in Nova Scotia commemorating her death, remembering her, praying for her, and asking her intercession for me. I had a profound experience of her presence.

In itself, this is not unusual—in the Roman Catholic tradition, we call it "the communion of saints"—because life is life and is happening all around us, even if we don't see it; it is not limited to this physical plane. So there I was, weeping over missing my mother, mourning the years we lost because of her emotional death at the time my brother died, and I had a profound experience of her presence and . . . a "message."

It was not a message in words—it was a complete experience. I understood it all at once in a kind of "whoosh." Someone once said, "Prayer is seeing all the connections." And in this one moment, sitting in the chapel, communing mysteriously with my mother, I saw all the "connections." I can't say, "Well, this happened first, and then that happened," because you lose all sense of time in these experiences; they take place in "eternity." But the message was simple and clear, even if it may sound strange to you: "Gaia, Samsara, and Narnia!"

But to receive a message like that is not the end of it. It is a very important part of living a contemplative life to sit with that experience over time, allowing it to grow deeper and deeper. And what I learned over time through my mother's heavenly experience was this: "I was your first Gaia teacher; I last saw you in Samsara; and now, one year later, I salute you and I celebrate the fullness of life from the Narnian realm ... on the other side of the door." And if you've read *The Chronicles of Narnia* by C. S. Lewis, you know the importance of "walking through the door" and what happens.

What I came to understand is that we experience life and death in three phases, which I call "Gaia, Samsara, Narnia" and which correspond in the Roman Catholic tradition to the Joyful Mysteries, the Sorrowful Mysteries, and the Glorious Mysteries of the Rosary.

TESSA BIELECKI

In the next discussion, Dr. Edward W. Bastian talks with Rabbi Zalman Schachter-Shalomi and Tessa Bielecki about alternative visions of Heaven, Hell, and Purgatory and their respective functions. Rabbi Zalman Schachter-Shalomi, whom we were first introduced to in Chapters 1 and 2, now reveals himself as one of the world's foremost authorities of Kabbalah —Jewish mysticism—and its teachings on the afterlife; Tessa Bielecki, a Carmelite Christian hermit and former abbess of the Spiritual Life Institute, speaks from the well of her own contemplative experiences and tells us what the Christian tradition has to say about them. Together, they explore the question: What happens to us when we die?   —*Ed.*

DR. EDWARD W. BASTIAN I would like to move on to a discussion of the afterlife; Reb Zalman, how do you look at the issue of an afterlife?

RABBI ZALMAN SCHACHTER-SHALOMI You know, when my son Yotam was a child, he said something really wonderful. You know how kids are: You put them to bed, you do the prayers with them, tell them a story, and they still don't want to let go. Then, just as you think they are about to go to sleep, they ask the kind of question that you can't resist! So one night Yotam said to me, "Abba, what happens when you die?" And I replied by asking, "What do *you* think?" Then he says, "Well, here's what I think; we have two lives. We have a wake-up life, and we have a dream life. I think the wake-up life stops, but the dream life continues." Wow!

If we can develop that life that people call the dream life—the place in which we dream, meditate, contemplate, and visualize—if that life can be enhanced, then we are already creating the landscape of our own survival. Similarly, my daughter, Shalvi, said to me one day, "Abba, when you're asleep, you can wake up. But when you're awake, can you wake up even more?" I have learned so much from my children. You see, all of this deals with consciousness, with awareness. Can we wake up even more? This waking up "even more" is one of the secrets of our survival after death.

DR. EDWARD W. BASTIAN But what is it that I want to wake up to?

RABBI ZALMAN SCHACHTER-SHALOMI We have a number of good words: "enlightenment," "salvation," "redemption." Most of the time, we think of these words as belonging only to the catechism, and we ignore them. But ask yourself, "What would 'redemption' be like? What would it really be like to be 'enlightened'? What would it really be like to be 'saved'? What would it really be like to be 'in the Light'?" My sense is that if we don't use our imagination, we aren't going to find our way *there* so easily. A lot depends on how you think about it.

Emmanuel Swedenborg[1] told a funny story in his book *Heaven and Hell.* Swedenborg was a scientist who began to have visions and revelations of other worlds. And in one of those visions he saw a squire and a group of his soldiers who had been killed in the Thirty Years War (a religious war between Catholics and Protestants) approaching St. Peter at the Pearly Gates, saying to St. Peter, "We fought in the war; please let us into Paradise." And St. Peter says to them, "Sure! You died in the religious war; you deserve Paradise. Would you please tell me, what is 'Paradise'?" The squire looks at his men confused and turns back to St. Peter, "Don't you know? . . . It's the harps!" So St. Peter calls back over his shoulder, "Number 2!" Then they let the squire and his soldiers into a room, lock them in, and they give them "the harps." After a very short time, the soldiers start banging on the doors, "Let us out of here; we can't stand it anymore!" And they hear a voice, saying, "But this is your Paradise." "No, no!" they cry, "This isn't Paradise!" "So what is?" "A church service!" they yell. So they let them into another room, and before long, they want to get out of there too. Finally, they say, "We don't know what Paradise is; would you please teach us?"

DR. EDWARD W. BASTIAN So your afterlife is what you make of it?

RABBI ZALMAN SCHACHTER-SHALOMI I believe so. You see, most people only have the smallest notion of what it is going to be like "in the Light," and as in this case, "the smallest notion" turned out to be too small. So dreaming is important. We have to dream bigger and with more sophistication. We don't want to get stuck in notions of the afterlife that are too limiting. Spend time daydreaming about the feeling you would like to experience in the afterlife rather than trying to determine the form of things. For instance, perhaps it will be like the feeling of a lovely summer day, lying on the wavy grass as a gentle breeze passes over you, feeling the earth hugging and supporting you. After all, it is that sense of having to support ourselves all the time that gives us our stress. If we really had faith in Divine Providence and how we are being cared for, we could really relax, and that is part of salvation too. *(See Zalman Schachter-Shalomi's* Doing Our Philosophical Homework *in "Exercises for Facing Our Mortality" on page 163.)*

If you have ever met someone who has really known a life beyond that of the physical body, you know that they behave differently than the ordinary person. My teacher, my *rebbe*,[2] Rabbi Joseph Isaac Schneersohn,[3] was such a person. In the 1920s, he was arrested by the Russian secret police, accused of "godly activity." And during the interrogation, one of the interrogators said to him, "You had better think about cooperating." The Rebbe just looked at him. Then, the man took out a gun and pointed it at the Rebbe, saying, "Many a man has changed his mind after meeting this 'persuader'!" The Rebbe simply replied, "Only a person who has many gods to serve and only one world to serve them in is threatened by your 'persuader.' But I who have only one God to serve and many Worlds to serve Him in—I'm not frightened."

Here he was, faced with a gun, but because he was so rooted in the knowledge and experience of other Worlds,[4] in those other bodies, he was able to be calm in the face of imminent death!

DR. EDWARD W. BASTIAN What about the "Hell" and "Purgatory" we have heard so much about in the West?

RABBI ZALMAN SCHACHTER-SHALOMI As you know, Tibetan Buddhists have a wonderful way of talking about the postmortem experience. In their language, they speak of the bardos, the states "in between."[5] When you read about them in the *Tibetan Book of the Dead*,[6] it sounds a little like Disneyland meets the House of Horrors! You go from one place to another, and creatures are jumping out to scare you—but even with the exotic imagery, there is really something to it, though not *exclusively* as depicted in the Tibetan Buddhist tradition. You see, a process of "purgation" happens in the afterlife, and it is the imagery that makes that process effective, but the imagery is not the process itself. The imagery is culturally determined, so what a Tibetan Buddhist may experience will not necessarily be the same as a Jew or a Christian's purgative imagery.

In the same way, consciousness is like tofu. It doesn't have its own taste. The taste of tofu depends on what you marinate it in. So if you ask yourself, "What is the marinade of my consciousness?" you have an idea of what a bardo is—an in-between place occupied by your consciousness. Just look at the places you often occupy with your consciousness: worry, concern, anger, and anxiety. Those are the mantras you meditate on when you wait for the doctor's office to call you.

Those states of consciousness are negative bardos, little hells filled with our private demons.

Who should be responsible for changing the marinade of consciousness if not ourselves? All the contemplative work we do is to create a different environment for consciousness. So think of the imaginable environments that you have inhabited as bardos in your life. And now imagine yourself passing out of the life of the body into the bardos you have created, all of the imaginal environments and consciousness states that have most occupied you in the body. *Oy!* There are some that you wish you hadn't brought with you, aren't there? If you don't change the "diapers" of your mind before passing out of this life, there is going to be some cleaning up that will be necessary on the other side, and it isn't going to feel good.

It is really necessary that we change the bardos that we inhabit in this life and live the divine promise, as it is given in the book of Deuteronomy: "I will give you that land that the Lord your God has promised you so that you might live heavenly days right here on this earth, *kiymay' hashamayim al ha'aretz.*"[7]

"If I were a rich man," I would broadcast in all media a positive bardo, an environment of peace and health. If that was out there, can you imagine the effect it would have on consciousness in the long term?

A man by the name of E. J. Gold[8] wrote a very interesting book called *The American Book of the Dead.*[9] It is both funny and frightening. Just imagine all of the senseless things that we have absorbed into our consciousness through the media and gossip, things that sit on the "hard drive" of our life memory. *Oy!* How can we get rid of them? We have to go to the "mind laundry." And that is what we call Purg-atory, the place where you do your purging, your cleaning up.

DR. EDWARD W. BASTIAN   This is a different take on Purgatory than most of us have heard—you are emphasizing the process—most people are usually taught and focused on the imagery and terror.

RABBI ZALMAN SCHACHTER-SHALOMI   It is the process that is important. Before the purgation, we will be *seen*, scrutinized— "Lord you have discerned and seen me, you have scanned me through and through from before the time You knitted me in my mother's womb, and You know my coming and going."[10] Sometimes when we look into one another's eyes, there comes a moment when we think, "I'd better not let him look further. He's going to see my garbage!" Right? Now, can you imagine if all that were to suddenly open up and become visible? Where are you going to hide it from the Ultimate Reality? So all these "files come up on the desktop," and the feeling that gives us is one of pain. And the question is, how do we treat that?

Most people are used to avoiding pain, doing almost anything not to encounter it, but the pain runs after them and gives them a very hard time. Once, before undergoing a surgical procedure, I went to see my hypnotherapist, and I asked her to make me a tape that I could hear on the way into the operating room that spoke to the deep part of my body, saying, "You are not being attacked; you are being helped . . . you are not being attacked; you are being helped. Everything that these people will be doing is to make you better and not to make you feel bad. Allow this to happen; it is all for healing." Can you imagine if the time comes for us that all those things that have to be shown and made clear of where we went wrong, where we were selfish, where we were cheating, where we told lies—when all that stuff starts coming up—and we will start to feel, "I don't want it! I don't want it!" but we are able to turn that around and say, "All right, bring it on; let me see it! This is all for my healing. This is to clean it up. The more I become aware of it, the more I can drop it. The more I fight it, the more it's going to pursue me." So you get the idea that when Dante[11] and other people were trying to describe what Purgatory is like, they described it according to their understanding of bardos. But the structure of purgation remains.

DR. EDWARD W. BASTIAN Is the harsh imagery necessary?

RABBI ZALMAN SCHACHTER-SHALOMI Well, it serves a purpose. But the images of Purgatory given us by Gustave Doré[12] and Hieronymus Bosch[13] only describe the Purgatory of their own imaginations. Now if you translate this into the inner feelings . . . what is this process of revealing and coming to terms with my karma like in the external world? Yes, it is as if I am being pulled on the rack, pinched, and prodded! "Why did I have to tell that useless lie? Why did I have to abuse anyone?" All this starts coming back, and if we can meet this, saying, "This is for our own good," because you can't put whipped cream on top of garbage and expect it to taste good. If we want to get to how beautiful Heaven will be, and if we want to go to the good places, we are not going to be able to enjoy that if we haven't cleaned up the filth we have accumulated. So you can understand the Hasidic master Reb Zushya of Anipol[14] who says, "If God will say to me, 'You're confined to *gehenna*,' to Purgatory, I'll say, 'Thank you God for the opportunity to clean up.' And I'll jump right in." *(See Zalman Schachter-Shalomi's* Giving Ourselves the Gift of Forgiveness *in "Exercises for Healing Emotional Wounds and Forgiveness" on page 173.)*

This is important to share not only because I am also preparing myself for the moment when that happens, but also because *age-ing* only becomes *sage-ing* as we come to terms with our own mortality, as we take account of our lives and temper our experiences against the knowledge of our eventual death. We have to do it if we are to become elders, and it is necessary for making a smooth transition out of this life and for taking our first steps into the beyond. I don't want to tell people, "Hey, once you die, there are only 'hallelujahs!' waiting for you on the other side; don't worry." There is a soul accounting that has to be done as a preparation in this life that has a bearing on the "audit" afterward.

DR. EDWARD W. BASTIAN You mentioned the bardos of the Tibetan Buddhist tradition before—is there something equivalent to the bardos, some equivalent process in the Jewish tradition?

RABBI ZALMAN SCHACHTER-SHALOMI Yes, there is a similar tradition in Judaism. We have the *Kaf ha-Kela*, "the Catapult." The Sages say that two angels stand at each end of the world and toss the soul from one to the other. It is almost as if the angels try to rid the soul of its accumulated psychic dust by putting it through a cosmic centrifuge until only pure soul remains! Without this treatment, the soul would be unable to silence all the sense-images and noises that were carried with it from this world and would have to wander in the world of *tohu* ("confusion") for ages. When this is done, we come to the Jewish idea of gehenna. Gehenna is not Hell, but also a Purgatory where the soul is purged from all defilements that it has accumulated during its life on Earth. And finally, when a soul is ready to enter Gan Eden (Paradise, literally the "Garden of Eden"), it must first be immersed in the River of

Light, created from the perspiration that flows from the heavenly hosts as they fervently sing glory to the Highest. This immersion is to empty the soul of any lingering Earth images, so that it may, without further illusion, see Heaven as it really is.[15]

DR. EDWARD W. BASTIAN The imagery of the River of Light immediately brings up the "Light" spoken of in near-death experiences.

RABBI ZALMAN SCHACHTER-SHALOMI This is the *Nahar DeNur*, the River of Light, mentioned in the book of Daniel,[16] in very traditional terms. When people talk about the "white light" they encounter in these near-death experiences, that is the River of Light we are speaking of. And what is it? Imagine yourself suddenly becoming transparent, like in *Star Trek*[17] when you are in the middle of the transporter cycle, and all you can see is the light-filled silhouette of yourself, insubstantial, and then the cycle completes, and you return to substantial existence and walk off the transporter pad. That feeling of waking up to the divinity that is really at the core of the core of the core of our being is what makes everything else pale. And so that is the River of Light. And several times we go through these experiences, and for some people who dread them, it feels terrible. And for some people who open themselves up to it and dip into that, it feels like that is the baptism that clears away all the sins for them.

Now, with that in mind, imagine that I steal a dollar, and in that moment, all I care for is the stolen dollar. But can you imagine what it would be like if suddenly I begin to see the consequences of that theft as they trickle down to people. When I look at the CEOs of these major corporations and health-care systems and the frauds they have committed, and think of the myriad ways these frauds have affected their employees and investors—imagine what it must be like for the former CEO who then sees and feels and experiences what it is like for thousands upon thousands of people to grow old and not to have insurance or a pension anymore! Can you imagine what it is like to be on the receiving end of that crime? How overwhelming that would be?

In this life, we only see what we see in this moment, but the results of the results of the results, the waves of the waves of the waves, we are not aware of. The higher our consciousness goes, and the more we become heavenly, the more we begin to see the results of the results of the results . . . and many of those are not so good and are even painful. So I don't think that there is fire or ice in Purgatory or Hell, or that they whip you with ribbons of fire, but I do believe that there is that experience of purgation.

That is one side of the situation. On the other side, after you have cleaned everything up, after experiencing it and dropping it, you can then see the results of the results of the results of the good that you did—I can imagine if someone who reads this actually does "die well," having been helped by something I said, I can imagine in my own afterlife being able to experience with them a glorious passing. I think I would enjoy that! Do you see what I'm saying? Getting to experience the results of the results of the results of the good. I think that is one idea of what Paradise is all about.

DR. EDWARD W. BASTIAN Reb Zalman has given us a glimpse of a different kind of Heaven and Hell than the one many of us got in Sunday school; does this agree with the Christian perspective, as you understand it, Tessa?

TESSA BIELECKI Yes, because most people have the wrong idea about Heaven. Heaven is a realm of being. I have actually talked to people who have had no interest in going to Heaven because of the "harps" Reb Zalman mentioned. Who wants to be in the "harp room" forever? I certainly don't! Nor do I want to be on a cloud or have wings for that matter. Heaven is not static; it is "dynamism without limit." Or as Reb Zalman's daughter suggested, it is "waking up within waking up." It is a constant waking up, a constant movement into more and more life.

DR. EDWARD W. BASTIAN Would you say something more about this?

TESSA BIELECKI Well, this is connected to what I said about my mother's death earlier, when I related it to the three phases of "Gaia, Samsara, and Narnia," which correspond in the Roman Catholic tradition to the Joyful Mysteries, the Sorrowful Mysteries, and the Glorious Mysteries.[18]

DR. EDWARD W. BASTIAN Yes, that was an interesting statement. If you don't mind, let me attempt to contextualize this for the readers before we continue. *Gaia* is referring to the Earth personified as goddess in Greek spirituality; *Samsara* to the Buddhist round of birth and rebirth, characterized by impermanence and suffering; and *Narnia* is referring to the imaginary land of C. S. Lewis's allegorical Christian children's stories.[19] Is that correct?

TESSA BIELECKI Yes. You see, we are born into the "Gaian realm." If we want to be biblical about it, we could say, Gaia, the Earth, is a garden, the Garden of Eden. And from the Christian point of view, Gaia speaks to the Mystery of Creation and Incarnation, where God is born into matter.

There are a great many saints who emphasize this, but two of my favorites are Hildegard of Bingen[20] and my friend, St. Teresa of Avila,[21] who said, "We are on the earth and clothed with it." For St. Teresa, matter *matters*. We also see this perspective in St. Francis of Assisi[22] in his beautiful canticle to "Brother Sun" and "Sister Moon." Francis wrote this at the end of his life, flat on his back, blind, and suffering from a serious gastrointestinal illness! And out of his profound inner experience, he sang to Brother Sun, Sister Moon! For me, knowing that has transformed my whole experience of this exquisite poem.

Likewise, there are beautiful psalms that describe the whole Gaian realm, where all of Creation is "praising God" and we are in communion with all of Creation. It is from this perspective that we can say that Gaia is Eden-esque, the joy of God in Creation, the incarnation of divinity!

Then we move into Samsara, the experience of the world as ephemeral and impermanent. In other words, all of this Gaian beauty and the experience of it is impermanent, fleeting, chang-ing . . . *dying*. We move into the realm of sorrow that corresponds to the passion, crucifixion, and death of Jesus, the Sorrowful Mysteries of the Rosary.[23] In truth, we are still in the Garden, but Paradise seems lost. We are exiled from Eden somehow. Jacques Maritain once called this life "a crucified paradise."[24]

So we start out in Eden, in Gaia, thinking this is Paradise, and then we realize, "Uh oh, something is wrong here; it is a crucified Paradise." Somehow the garden is spoiled. It has been invaded. In the New Testament, Jesus uses the image of weeds sown among the wheat. When people say, "Well, let's pull them up," he says, "No, leave the weeds," they are part of the context.[25]

The story of Adam and Eve describes what went wrong. You cannot say it didactically, but we have this beautiful story, which simply says, "Wow, somehow we messed up; something went wrong." We Catholics also have a beautiful hymn that we sing regularly, especially in the monastic tradition, "Salve Regina," "Hail, Holy Queen." Several lines talk about our being the "poor, banished children of Eve." That's how we suffer in Samsara—as the poor, banished children of Eve, "mourning and weeping in this valley of tears."

St. Teresa of Avila has a more humorous, edgy way of describing Samsara, which I think is terrific. She says this life is like "a night in a bad inn," of which she had many. Once her cart broke down, and she was wallowing in the mud trying to fix the wheel when she said to God, "Look, if this is the way you treat your friends, no wonder you have so few of them." That's Samsara! But, that is also a prayer. We have to broaden our sense of what we mean by prayer.

My mother died "crucified" to her dialysis machine. If you have ever seen anyone on dialysis, it is a very dramatic cruciform position, and for my mother, it was extremely painful. Another painful part of that ordeal for me was that for over a month I had nursed her (along with my sister and my father). And when my mother's doctor said she was stable, I left to go to my Nova Scotia monastery, where I was needed at the time. Within twenty-four hours—though I had been there every step of the way up to then—she died. I had to ask, "Why? Why when I had been there every minute was I not there for that moment?" So I last saw her in Samsara, as the message I received in the chapel said.

And this brings us to Narnia. If you have ever read *The Chronicles of Narnia*, you know they are a good read, and for those of us who are Christian, and who may have become disaffected or disillusioned, they are a good way to reexperience Christianity. In my own experience, these fairy tales speak to you just as well if you are seven, thirty, fifty, or even, I suspect, eighty years old. This is because they come from the mythopoeic[26] experience, that archetypal level that goes so deep that no matter how simple the words, the experience of primal imagery and symbols makes it profoundly human and significant. Carl Jung[27] says, if you're struck by an image, boy, you should pay attention to that because it is some signal to you that there is something really important here. C. S. Lewis is full of that.

DR. EDWARD W. BASTIAN And what does Narnia signify for you?

TESSA BIELECKI Narnia is "eternal," it is "glory," and it corresponds to the resurrection of Jesus, the Glorious Mysteries of the Rosary. The important thing here is that glory *is not* joy. Glory is what we experience when we have been through the sorrow of Samsara, and the joy and sorrow come together in something so profound, so mysterious, a whole other world opens up.

It is not the experience of Gaia. It is something much higher and deeper after having been through a tremendous amount of pain. It is also important to understand what I mean by the word "eternal." Again, I have talked to people who say, "Oh gosh, if Heaven is eternal, I want out!" because they have this sense that it is going to be the same thing all the time, and it is going to be boring. But eternity is not perpetuity; it is a point. It is that mysterious point where past, present, and future all come together, where everything comes together. In a way, it is indescribable. And this is what happens to us in contemplative experience. This is what happens to us in our prayer. This is what happens to us in our meditation. We touch that place where past, present, and future all come together, where we touch eternity . . . and where eternity touches us. I was taught a little Latin saying that helps me keep things in perspective, *Quid est ad aeternitatem?*, "What is it in the light of eternity?"

The important point is that this Narnian realm does not occur exclusively *after* death. It happens now. It happens here. We know it if we can "wake up within waking up." That is the "resurrection" we can experience if we would only die dead enough—we could move into this whole other realm of being.

SEVEN

Life *After* Life?

*From life to pass into death
—this is our experience,
this is what we see.
Through death
to pass into life—
This is the mystery.*

POPE JOHN PAUL II

A PERSONAL EXPERIENCE

ONE SUNDAY NIGHT, I didn't feel much like being a canasta dummy, so I said to my friend Bill, "Come on, let's do something else." Movies were not available on Sundays then (the 1950s), there were "blue laws" in Massachusetts, so we looked in the paper and saw an advertisement for a Spiritualist Church. It was starting at seven o'clock, and it it was about 6:30 p.m. as we made up our minds. So we hopped in the car and drove over there in about fifteen minutes. We got to the place, and there was this nice lady with gray hair and deep eyes greeting us at the door. I asked her, "What do you do here?" So she says, "You take a little piece of paper and you write out your question to 'the spirit,' put it into a basket, and you donate a quarter." So we did that and went downstairs in the basement room, which wasn't very big, and we sat down in some folding chairs.

Agnes Taylor was the name of the "channel." She was a spiritualist minister who also attended an Anglican church, and for a while, she was playing a reed organ upstairs; "Nearer My God to Thee," "Lead Kindly Light," "Abide with Me"—you know, the regular hymns. And then she comes down and is introduced by the president. She steps up on the dais and says, "I am not a mentalist," and so on. And, as she is talking, she is going more and more into her trance, and finally begins to speak about herself in the third person with her voice slightly changed: "Mrs. Taylor is just our channel for what is going on." She goes over to the basket and feels strong vibrations in one or another billet, and picks my billet on which I had written a silly question, because I didn't take this seriously. So she says, "You sir," and points to me. "Behind you there is a woman standing. She has a kerchief down to her eyes, and she has her hands folded, and she looks at you with great love. She is standing at the entrance between a small pantry and the kitchen, and you are swaying back and forth with a blanket that has white and black stripes on it wrapped around you, and you have your back against the window. There is a blue book in your hand," exactly describing my *siddur* (prayer book).

The scene she described was when my daughter Mimi was born, and I didn't go to *shul* (synagogue) that morning, so I could go to my wife in the hospital, which was quite a trek. And she was describing my mother-in-law standing there and watching me with great joy. You know, a new grandchild and a rabbi in the household. She loved me a lot.

Her message was what she always would say, "Don't worry; things are going to be good. You are going to get a letter," and so on, nothing very evidential. But then, Mrs. Taylor said, "The woman's name is . . . Kh . . . Kh . . . Khannah." She was having trouble pronouncing the Hebrew gutturals in the name Hannah, which was my mother-in-law's name. I was flabbergasted.

She then went on with the other people, saying, "Somebody . . . his name was Tom. I see a mark on his neck. I don't know whether he hung himself or cut his own throat." And then she says something about suicides having a hard time because they remain earth-bound for a long time. She tells someone else, "You should not have your trial in Providence, but in Newport." And then she said to someone else, "There is a blue light already out; your mother has been called; she will go within a month." She was reading the whole group and finally she comes to my friend Bill, and she says, "I see a young woman here; she is about ten or eleven. She has curls like Shirley Temple. She was killed in an automobile accident." Well, my heart nearly stopped, because it was a perfect description of his daughter. He grabs my hand and says, "Relax." It was his sister who was killed in an automobile accident some years ago. Boom, bull's-eye!

Then she goes on to say to Bill, "There is a man standing behind you, sir. He is your father, and he has been trying to get in touch with you all these years. You and your wife went to the movies, and he was babysitting with your daughter and your son. When you came home from the movie, he was slumped in the chair with a heart attack, and your baby son was on the floor crying. He has been trying to tell you, even if you had been home, being a heart specialist, you couldn't have helped because it was a massive heart attack. And he wanted you to know not to feel guilty for that. He enjoyed spending the last half-hour of his life holding his grandson in his arms." I was overwhelmed. It was a powerful thing, so you can imagine how I was shaken. All of that had been true of Bill.

So, a little while later, I visited Mrs. Taylor at her house with my wife, and she said, "Play me something on the organ." I played a Hasidic *niggun* (melody), and she got up from the chair and said, "There is a man here. He is from the twentieth plane. He is wearing a round fur hat," and she went on describing my *rebbe* (spiritual master), Rabbi

Joseph Isaac Schneersohn, who had recently passed. And she says, "He is sending his blessing." I wouldn't have dared to come to her with the Rebbe in mind, but that niggun that I played, the whole thing, was calling him. It was an amazing experience.

RABBI ZALMAN SCHACHTER-SHALOMI

I n this section, Dr. Edward W. Bastian talks with Dr. Marilyn Schlitz about current scientific research on nonlocal consciousness and the afterlife. Dr. Schlitz is the vice president for Research and Education at the Institute of Noetic Sciences, senior scientist at the Research Institute, California Pacific Medical Center, and a congressionally appointed member of the Advisory Council of the Office of Alternative Medicine and the National Center for Complementary and Alternative Medicine at the National Institutes of Health. Here, Dr. Schlitz discusses the possibility that consciousness *may* extend beyond the confines of the physical body. — *Ed.*

DR. EDWARD W. BASTIAN At this point, I would like to invite Dr. Marilyn Schlitz of the Institute of Noetic Sciences[1] into the discussion to talk about the afterlife from a scientific perspective . . . though, I suppose some would consider that an oxymoron?

DR. MARILYN SCHLITZ This question of what happens when we die or what is the nature of consciousness is really sort of a mystery-at-large. We can have dreams and visions, we can have plans for the future, but ultimately there is that final question mark at the end of life. What happens? And this issue is, I think, one of the most profound, if not *the* most profound issue facing humanity. It takes us from the most intimate to the ultimate aspects of our experience. Intimate, being those aspects of interiority and subjectivity that are so close to who we are, that are so personal to each of us; and the ultimate being those greater truths that have yet to be revealed—the domain of science, the attempt to understand the irregularities of nature. And this question, "What happens to consciousness after we die?" provides us a fundamental gateway into understanding the interface, or the meeting place between the intimate, the ultimate, the effable, and the ineffable.

Every culture throughout recorded history has had a body of practices and beliefs related to the issue of how our consciousness either does or does not transcend bodily death. But how can science say something to us about something that is so profoundly cultural and spiritual? How do we begin to reconcile a faith in science and objectivity with this notion of a transitory state of consciousness?

There are various domains of evidence. There are lab studies that provide evidence for the idea that consciousness may be something more than the brain itself, something that transcends the brain. Then there are specific case studies. But none of these data points, in and of themselves, provide *conclusive* evidence of the survival of consciousness after bodily death.

What you find as you begin to amass the evidence is a compelling case for *at least considering* the possibility that science has something to say, and that, in fact, there may be an ontological basis for beginning to understand some of these claims and practices from a Western scientific point of view. It is not science in the sense of prediction and control, but it is an attempt to begin to understand whether it is chicanery, fraud, delusion, or something that can actually be corroborated based on some systematic inquiry into the nature of these kinds of experiences.

DR. EDWARD W. BASTIAN So how do you even begin to try to establish "nonlocal consciousness" in a scientific setting?

DR. MARILYN SCHLITZ One method is through studying "mediumship," as we heard about in Reb Zalman's story. Now mediumship pretty much went away as a cultural practice (as well as a scientific interest) many years ago. And it is only within the last few years that scientists (Dean Radin[2] at IONS, and Gary Schwartz[3] at the University of Arizona) have begun to look at ways you could begin to study mediumship under controlled circumstances.

What Gary's been doing, for example, is bringing self-professed mediums together with people who have lost a loved one. In these experiments, only the medium is allowed to speak. And what Gary has done is develop a method by which you can compare the report by the medium with the correct reading and three others, bringing an objective approach to what is a very subjective experience. Using this method, they are attempting to corroborate how the medium's communication matched the experience that they had of their departed loved one. Again, it is a way of beginning to bring a scientific perspective to bear on that age-old and profoundly mysterious question.

DR. EDWARD W. BASTIAN What experiments have been done in your lab? And have they supported the idea of nonlocal consciousness?

DR. MARILYN SCHLITZ We look at the evidence from our experiments as data points contributing to a larger case, making the argument for survival of consciousness after death perhaps more plausible.

Some of the research happening at the Institute of Noetic Sciences has to do with nonlocal healing and nonordinary communications. The nonlocal healing, or distance healing work, has been done in a variety of different situations—both in a basic science perspective, where we work with cell cultures and petri dishes, with animal and human physiology, and in clinical trials that have looked at the possibility that one person's consciousness or intention can actually influence the physiological activity of another person at a distance.

In order to do this—again, if you are trying to make an argument that there is something that goes against the dominant scientific paradigm—you need to rule out conventional sensory explanations. From a scientific point of view, what we are trying to do is build the best case we can. And so we developed a protocol or a methodology in which we could rule out all the kinds of conventional sensory exchanges that occur between two people.

We identified in the distant healing research a particular aspect of physiology that we could measure. We also used a random sequence and statistical analysis.

We invite somebody to come into our lab, and we monitor their autonomic nervous system activity, that part of the physiology that functions automatically. And then we have a healer ("sender") in another room who attempts to influence the distant person at random times throughout the session. Meanwhile, we have a researcher who is monitoring the whole situation from a third room.

The receiver, the recipient of this distant healing, is put in a two-thousand-pound electromagnetically shielded room, where they sit in a comfortable chair, and we monitor their electrodermal activity, the skin conductance in the hand (the same procedure they use for lie-detector tests and galvanic skin response). We're able to measure their physiology over, say, a thirty-minute period.

DR. EDWARD W. BASTIAN You've clearly taken extreme measures using a two-thousand-pound "black box"; has this garnered any respect for the validity of your experiments in the wider scientific community?

DR. MARILYN SCHLITZ I think more respect has come from our willingness to accept criticism. Many people don't like to be critiqued, but we feel it is good thing, because if we can identify potential weaknesses in our protocols, then we strengthen the case we are building in the future.

When we were building our lab at the Institute of Noetic Sciences, we invited Stefan Schmidt, a German psychophysiologist who did his doctoral thesis critiquing research that we had done, to the United States to help us set it up. We also invited Richard Wiseman, a leading skeptic, to help us make sure we did not have any sensory leakage that could refute our findings. So the protocol and the design of the laboratory are very clean. And as I said, this two-thousand-pound electromagnetically shielded room rules out any kind of conventional communication that could happen between two people.

You might wonder why I was so compulsive about all this, but there are a number of people who love to debunk these kinds of studies. Our goal was to make sure we weren't deceiving ourselves and weren't being deceived by the people who would come into the lab. We felt it was important to rule out any kind of conventional electromagnetic communication that could happen between the two people.

In this protocol, the subject's image appears on a closed-circuit television while he or she sits in a quiet room for twenty or thirty minutes—it varies depending on the experiment. At the same time you have a healer in another room, at a distance, who is seeing the subject's image by a closed-circuit television at random periods of time. The job of the healer is to try to get the subject's attention during the "staring period" and not during the "control period."

In this way, we can actually collect data that allows us to look at that whole thirty-minute period and then to divide that thirty-minute period into "sampling epochs" or "measurement periods." We can assess the average amount of autonomic nervous system activity during these different sampling periods. We found that the autonomic nervous system activity was aroused (was actually significantly greater during the staring period as compared to the control period). So it provides a way of objectively measuring the impact of intention on the physiology of another person. And again, most cultures have the belief that there are practitioners who can use their minds and their intentions to help or hinder a person at a distance. And now we find it in the scientific tradition. And so, yes, this is significant.

DR. EDWARD W. BASTIAN Even couched in the language of "statistical significance," that's an amazing statement; the subtle world of spirituality shows up on a scientific graph!

DR. MARILYN SCHLITZ As Florence Nightingale[4] once said, "God is revealed through statistics." What she meant by this is that there is a pattern to nature that is revealed as the scientist seeks to measure it. Still, what we are studying is a mix between the objective world and the subjective experience of the practitioners. There is a cartoon of a scientist next to a genie coming out of his test tube, and because scientists like objectivity, and they don't like these extraneous variables, he says, "Go away, you fool. You just ruined my experiment!" In our lab, we actually try to invite the genie in rather than excluding it from the lab.

We did a series of experiments in this "staring paradigm" in which we found statistically significant evidence for this nonlocal communication.

I have a colleague, Dr. Richard Wiseman, who is a card-carrying member of the skeptical community. He is a professional magician and psychologist, and I think an open-minded skeptic. The word "skeptic" actually comes from the Greek, meaning "an open-minded person." The dogmatists were the ones who asserted things and thought they knew. The skeptics were the ones who stayed open. And the term has become somewhat muddled with debunking. But in this case, it is holding a suspension of belief more than a disbelief. Anyway, Dr. Wiseman did these same experiments in his lab in England and, in fact, found *no evidence* at all for a significant difference in these two sets of conditions. The question then became, is there something different about the way I'm running my experiments as compared to what he is doing? And in science, the objectivity of the investigator is critical. It is one of the cornerstones of how we build science. So to somehow demonstrate that an experimenter's intention can have some influence on the outcome of his or her experiment has pretty revolutionary consequences for the ways in which we do science. It seemed important for us to look at why were we getting these differences.

We decided to do a formal experiment in his laboratory, under *his* conditions. It was the identical protocol, subject population, equipment, randomization; everything was identical except that I worked with half the people, and he worked with half the people. And what we found at the end of the experiment was that we had both replicated our original findings. I had found significant evidence of a nonlocal communication, while he had found none. What is happening here? What does this say about objectivity, and how does this begin to challenge some of the assumptions we are making about how science can operate? And also, what is the power of our consciousness?

Then we brought the experiment to my lab and did two identical parallel experiments. Once again, both of us replicated our original findings. This suggests not only that some kind of nonlocal exchange of information can occur here that provides support for the notion that intention or prayer can actually have a physically measurable affect on someone at a distance, but also that the intention and belief systems of the investigators themselves may have some bearing on the outcome of the studies! We later conducted a third experiment, but in this study, the results were not as clear-cut as in the previous two. What *is* clear is that this is a challenging but ultimately promising area for research.

DR. EDWARD W. BASTIAN What about near-death experiences?

DR. MARILYN SCHLITZ Bruce Greyson, a psychiatrist at the University of Virginia, described a near-death experience that appears to be one of the best cases of evidence for some non-local consciousness. In a recording he made, he described the case of a woman with a large aneurysm at the base of her brain that was almost impossible to get at without rupturing it. If the aneurysm bursts, you bleed to death rapidly. So the woman underwent an unusual procedure called "hypothermic cardiac arrest" in which they drained the blood out of her body so that there is no risk of this aneurysm rupturing. Then they could safely correct it surgically.

The problem is that you usually can't survive without blood going to your brain. So they cooled her body down first to 60 degrees Fahrenheit. That slows the brain metabolism down, so you can survive longer periods of time. The operation typically takes forty-five to sixty minutes, and many people cannot survive at 60 degrees.

They closed her eyes and put tape over them so that her eyes wouldn't dry out. They also put molded speakers in her ears that were constantly emitting a 100-decibel click, which is the level of a loud orchestra, so that they could determine if the response in the brain stem was no longer functioning. She was isolated in terms of vision and hearing from the outside world and completely anesthetized.

They cut into the femoral artery in her groin, drained her blood out from there into a heart-lung pump, which was encased in an ice bath. They cooled the blood down, put it back into her vein, and circulated it to cool her body down. Then, when her body got down to 60 degrees, her heart stopped from the shock. They then turned the pump off and tilted the surgical table up so that the blood drained out. So there was no more blood in her brain, no heart beat, no respiration. The EEG[5] was totally flat. The response in her brain stem to the auditory clicks stopped. By every crite-rion we have, this woman was *dead*.

During this procedure, this woman reports that she "woke up." As far as everyone else was concerned, she was still uncon-scious. But she woke up. She heard a sound that, as a professional musician, she recognized as a natural D. That was the saw they were using to cut her skull open. She heard a woman's voice talk-ing about a problem with the right femoral artery and having to use the left. She saw the very unusual type of bone saw they were using to cut her skull open. She watched the procedures for a while and then got distracted—as people often do in near-death experiences—by a tunnel of light and deceased relatives. She had reunions with several relatives. Eventually, she was told she had to come back. She came back to her body, reluctantly, and witnessed what was going on in the operating room again and remembered the music that was playing in the operating room that she later mentioned to the surgeons.

So here was a report of a near-death experience with accu-rate perceptions from an out-of-body perspective of things that were not just lucky guesses. She described events and objects in precise detail! She reported communication with deceased rela-tives and also described her thinking as being much clearer and faster than it ever had been while she was alive. All these things were happening while she had no blood in her body, obviously no heartbeat, no breathing, and no brain waves, either from the surface EEG or the deep electrodes in her brain stem. You cannot get much more dead than that—and yet her consciousness was very much aware.

EIGHT

Afterlife and Reincarnation Reconsidered

I could well imagine that I might have lived in former centuries and there encountered questions I was not yet able to answer; that I had to be born again because I had not fulfilled the task that was given to me. When I die, my needs will follow along with me—that is how I imagine it. I will bring with me what I have done. In the meantime it is important to ensure that I do not stand at the end with empty hands.

CARL JUNG
Memories, Dreams, Reflections

IT'S LATER THAN YOU THINK

SEVERAL YEARS AGO now, I had a year of profound loss; I actually lost fifteen friends in one year, and one of them was very special and dear to me—Elisabeth Targ. She had been one of my oldest friends and colleagues.

One evening I was driving with my five-year-old son and noticing the full moon. I said, "Look, Skyler. Look at that full moon; isn't this a glorious night to be alive?"

He looked at the moon and asked me, "Mommy, do you think that dead people can't see the full moon?"

I said, "Well, maybe not; maybe dead people can't see the full moon."

Then he said, "Oh, no, Mommy; that's not true at all. Elisabeth is up there right now, and she's watching the full moon, and she's singing, 'Enjoy yourself, it's later than you think . . . enjoy yourself, it's later than you think.'"

I turned around, and I looked at him, and I thought, "Well, that's a good lesson."

DR. MARILYN SCHLITZ

I n the pages that follow, Dr. Edward W. Bastian talks with Dr. Marilyn Schlitz and Rabbi Zalman Schachter-Shalomi, respectively, about the scientific view of reincarnation and reincarnation in the Jewish tradition. Dr. Marilyn Schlitz is the coauthor of *Consciousness and Healing: Integral Approaches to Mind-Body Medicine* (with Tina Amorok and Marc Micozzi), and Rabbi Zalman Schachter-Shalomi is the coauthor of *A Heart Afire: Stories and Teachings of the Early Hasidic Masters* (with Netanel Miles-Yepez). Here, Dr. Schlitz gives a précis of some scientific research being carried out on reincarnation, while Rabbi Schachter-Shalomi discusses different perspectives on reincarnation in the mystical tradition of Judaism.   — *Ed.*

DR. EDWARD W. BASTIAN And what does science think of reincarnation, Marilyn?

DR. MARILYN SCHLITZ Even in our materialistic culture, this idea that consciousness may survive bodily death is very prevalent—67 percent of Americans believe in the survival of consciousness. Further, they believe that the after-death experience will take the form of a journey into other planes of reality.

The work that was done by Ian Stevenson[1] at the University of Virginia on this is monumental. For about thirty years he collected case reports of possible evidence for reincarnation. He had a very elaborate procedure for getting information that could verify or corroborate the experience. And within his database the most compelling subgroup of those case collections are what are called the "biological markers subgroup." These are cases in which a young child is born with a birth defect or some kind of abnormality that matches with the identity or the personality that the young child is reporting to have been.

Now most of these biological markers of reincarnation correlate with fatal wounds on the previous person. And in fact, Stevenson in his case collection has sixty-two cases with very good medical corroboration. One case of his comes from Turkey. In this example, there are two birthmarks associated with this possible reincarnation. The person who was believed to be the primary personality died of gunshot wounds that went up through his chin and out of his skull. And so when he died, there were two wounds. There was a man who had an experience of being that personality and felt that he had different aspects or characteristics of that personality. And there was a wound that was associated with the gunshot entry. Initially, that was really all they had to go on. They did not feel that it was a particularly strong case until Stevenson had the idea to check for a second mark, corresponding to the exit wound. Stevenson predicted that if this was the correct reincarnation, there should also be a scar on his head—which in fact they found. And the scar was a smaller scar that reflected the exit of the gunshot. Now again, these are compelling cases that are well documented, but whether you treat them as evidential is really up to you.

Another documented case was of a man who was dying and unconscious, and his wife used greasy soot from a cooking pot to mark a line around the front part of his left ankle. And then a child was born who had this birthmark in the family and who was identified as the reincarnation. So this is another example where there was actually some corroboration at those multiple levels.

But the one I find most interesting comes from Nigeria. And this is what is called an experimental birth defect case. Now, many people in West Africa believe that if one mutilates the body of a dead infant, then a defect occurring in another child will allow recognition of the reincarnation. So if an infant dies, they want to know that the reincarnation has occurred. And this practice derives from another belief fostered by high infant mortality that there are a band of spirits who are born, die quickly, are born again, die again, over and over again, and that they do this to harass parents. And that the only way to break the cycle is to inflict some sort of injury on the dead baby's body since this will produce a defect on the next body, which repels the spirit. So usually parents do something fairly minor: they'll clip off the end of a fingertip, for example.

In this case, a father, who apparently had lost many infants, became so angry at the death of the last one that he cut off all the fingers and toes, tied the legs together with a rope as a symbolic gesture to prevent the spirits from walking, and then hung the cut-off fingers and toes in a bag in his house intended to ward off the spirits from ever returning to the house. He then married another wife. She knew nothing about this bag that was hanging above the door for eleven years, during which time she had three normal children. They were then doing some renovation in the house. Someone cut down the bag, and the father was very alarmed when he learned this had happened. But apparently he didn't tell the wife. Their next child was born with serious birth defects, apparently reflecting the postmortem mutilation of the previous child.

So how do we explain these possible reincarnation cases? There are normal explanations for birth defects: Are they just chance correspondences in which there happened to be some synchronicity between these events? Is there something that happens in the mother's body that she, through her own psychic ability, is somehow able to cause changes in the fetus before it is born? Or are these evidential of some aspect of survival of personality following bodily death? I don't think that we can completely answer this, but in each case, it provides another data point for reading. An excellent book on this topic is called *Irreducible Mind: Toward a Psychology for the 21st Century* by Edward F. Kelly, Emily Williams Kelly, Adam Crabtree, and Alan Gauld; it provides a complete review of this literature in this area.

DR. EDWARD W. BASTIAN Reb Zalman, are there any teachings about reincarnation in the Jewish tradition?

RABBI ZALMAN SCHACHTER-SHALOMI Yes. In Judaism, or Jewish mysticism, reincarnation is spoken of as *gilgul*. Gilgul is a "wheel," a cycle. Sometimes it is said that gilgul is the result of "incompletes" in the last life that you have to come back and fix up.

Nothing new can be gained in Heaven, so the quantity of *mitzvot* (deeds or blessings) and Torah[2] acquired by the time of death is what remains with a person after death. In Heaven, one can gain only a deeper and richer understanding of one's life on Earth. It is for this reason that souls, once they have absorbed all that Heaven has to offer, apply for reincarnation in order to attain further perfection. Reincarnation is also granted to allow the soul to bring about a restitution of the wrongs it has committed.

This is the point: sometimes you have to come and see the results of what you left behind the last time around. And so, reincarnation is sometimes not such a good thing. On the other hand—there is always an "on the other hand"—there is a situation sometimes where something is needed here on the planet or an opportunity has arisen that has not arisen before. And there are some of our mystics who say reincarnation does not always go according to the regular temporal line. Therefore, you can have a reincarnation in the future that you need first before you can have a reincarnation in the past.

I have also had experiences with people whose last breath was in the gas chambers and who have come back with those terrible imprints. A student of mine, Yonassan Gershom, wrote the book *Beyond the Ashes* documenting the cases of people who have come back, some of them saying, "Never again, we want to either heal the planet or we want to heal justice. We want to make sure that this will not happen again!"[3]

Another reincarnation situation in Judaism occurs in moments of great danger, when the disembodied come to forewarn their loved ones through dreams and visions, helping them through trials and temptations. A soul is said to have come into *ibbur* (literally, "pregnancy") when it enters—in a benign fashion—the body and soul of a person living here on Earth. Often such an ibbur can raise a person to great heights, temporarily. Ibbur, however, can also help the discarnate soul who is in need of only one *mitzvah* (deed carried out to fulfill God's commandments) in order to round out a particular incarnation. Instead of risking the danger of another incarnate existence, it can receive the needed merit from the living by helping someone as an ibbur. The custom of naming children after the deceased is a means of affording the departed another return to life or of creating affinities so that it, as an ibbur, may help their offspring and receive help in return.

Reincarnation is an option at any point after gehenna (Purgatory). The process repeats until a soul has completely built its spiritual body. Yet even the completion of the spiritual body is not the ultimate state of being. Having attained such fullness, a soul can be "absorbed into the very Body of the King," the ultimate aim of its yearning and longing. Thus the soul merges finally into God as a drop in the Ocean.

DR. EDWARD W. BASTIAN Do we need to mourn then?

RABBI ZALMAN SCHACHTER-SHALOMI Mourning is for us, but many of the customs of mourning have developed in order to assist the soul through its many trials in the afterlife. The reciting of the mourners' Kaddish,[4] it is said, helps to "cool the fires of gehenna." The maximum sentence for this purgatory is twelve months; however, the mourners' Kaddish is only recited for eleven months, so as not to insult the dead by implying that he or she would have to serve the full term!

Likewise, each year on the *yahrzeit* (anniversary of death), a higher rung of Gan Eden (Paradise) is achieved by the soul. While the soul celebrates its "birthday into Heaven" with its celestial friends, the living traditionally celebrate the *aliyat ha-neshamah* ("ascendancy of the soul") by praying for a more exalted position in Heaven for that soul.

Since souls are incapable of acquiring new merit after death, the living can transfer "credit to the account" of a loved one, thus enabling it to achieve higher levels. One of the most potent means is by offering *tzedakah* ("charity") in the name of the deceased.

NINE

Final Thoughts:
The Concluding Dialogue

In death we are most disposed to respond to the divine summons and achieve our destiny with a total affirmation of our entire being. In that undivided and undistracted moment, we encounter Christ completely and with all our being say "yes" to the sovereign claim of God, to all the exigencies of love. The opportunity occurs not after death, when our eternal destiny is already fixed, nor before death in the debilitating state of dying; but in death. In that moment when the soul leaves the body (not really the body but the corpse), it awakens suddenly to its pure spirituality and reaches the complete unity of its being. Then we are free to decide for Christ or against him. Death, then, is rebirth.

WILLIAM MCNAMARA, O.C.D.
Christian Mysticism: The Art of the Inner Way

A CONSCIOUS DEATH

I ACTUALLY WANTED to be conscious through my dying, as Reb Zalman had brought up. So as I was lying in the emergency room, having been left alone for a long time unattended, my mind started alternating between three parallel tracks: letting my kids know,[1] getting good medical attention,[2] and my spiritual practice. I was operating in a very focused, almost businesslike way while I was lying there, and I was really trying to be in meditation as I was doing these three things. The doctor had already told me that the embolism might very well land in the wrong place in my lungs, and if that happened, he wouldn't be able to stop it, and I would die. So my primary attitude was that I had work to do meditatively to be ready for that moment.

Three days later, I was released from the hospital, and I was staying back with the sisters at La Casa De Maria, sleeping in the same room that had been occupied by both Father Thomas Keating and Thomas Merton. At about midnight I began to experience pain in my chest again, and I considered it a distinct possibility that I might not see the morning. I took it as a great opportunity to focus on my meditation and other practices I had learned from our great teachers.

So I began to write a note to the people who would find my body and a letter to my children, Jonathan and Alexandra. I remembered what Joan and Ira had said about this during the Living-Fully seminar, and I was much more conscious now of the effect my death might have on others; I felt that I needed to be considerate of them and to make things as easy for them as possible. Already between the seminar and this second near-death experience, I had redone my will, I had given away a lot of my belongings, I had pared down the amount of possessions I had, and I had already simplified my life a lot. I got rid of papers and junk that I didn't want my kids to have to deal with if I died.

It was all very practical stuff, but it was certainly a spiritual process to deal with it. Ira's "four things that matter most"—forgive me, I forgive you, thank you, and I love you—were very important in the letter I wrote to my children, and I had been trying to do this work quite consciously ever since I had heard him speak of these things.

DR. EDWARD W. BASTIAN

In the following discussion, Tina L. Staley, the director of Pathfinders National, takes Dr. Edward W. Bastian's place as interviewer and talks with all of the assembled teachers and experts about the possible relationships between their respective disciplines around the issues of living fully and dying well. Dr. Bastian is now introduced as the founder and president of the Spiritual Paths Foundation and the Spiritual Paths Institute, a Tibetan Buddhist of the Gelugpa School, former member of the Snowmass Interreligious Conference, and Ph.D. in Buddhist Studies and Western Philosophy from the University of Wisconsin. —*Ed.*

TINA L. STALEY I want to start off by asking you a question, Ed. Since you have already faced a night in which you thought you were going to die, I think it would be useful for everyone if you would tell us more about what you were doing that night to deal with this and why.

DR. EDWARD W. BASTIAN Well, after I had finished my note about what to do with my body and had written the letter to my children, I turned to basic Buddhist practices; I began to meditate on compassion and emptiness, bringing my consciousness to my heart chakra,[3] visualizing my next life and the bodhisattva-like being[4] I would like to be reincarnated as . . . and I was praying! But mostly I was just trying to keep my consciousness in that meditative state, so that if I died, it would be a seamless transition.

TINA L. STALEY Can you explain why it is useful for a Buddhist to meditate on emptiness at the moment when you are going to die?

DR. EDWARD W. BASTIAN The word "*shunyata*," or "emptiness," has a very specific definition and context in Buddhism. Through it, I understand that my body, my consciousness, and all things in my experience are lacking in inherent or permanent existence; it is also bound up with the understanding of the interdependence and impermanence of all things taught in Buddhism. So meditating on emptiness is, to my mind, a supreme *via negativa*, or apophatic spiritual practice,[5] in that it forces me to look critically at all of the contents of my experience, which in the end are found to be wholly ephemeral.

This is important because when you are face-to-face with your own fears, anxieties, pains, or even dreamlike perceptions at the time of death, meditating on emptiness allows you to have a certain distance or detachment. Whatever your perceptions, you are not going to think of them as real and as having their own existence or having any inherent power to affect you. Whether a beautiful or an ugly image, you need not be attached or drawn into it. By meditating on emptiness, you are not swept away or distracted, attracted or repulsed. With a clear mind, you are able to see whatever it is that appears before you for what it actually is—*an appearance*.

So emptiness is a really important thing to cultivate in meditation, and especially important at the time of death, because what is happening then can be quite scary, and you need to *be there*, and not be carried away by fears and anxieties . . . far away from what your wish or goals for that moment would be.

TINA L. STALEY And how does this relate to your meditation on compassion and transitioning to a "bodhisattva-like" state?

DR. EDWARD W. BASTIAN Because you have already cultivated a clear mind, you are able to meditate on compassion more effectively; no matter what it is that you see or experience, your first reaction to that will be compassion, and you are not being drawn away from it because it has a horrific or a beautiful appearance, whatever it may be. You are not being attached to it, and then you are able to apply a conscious compassion to it . . . not an emotionally "hooked" reaction. So if you are then trying to create for yourself a rebirth—which is in some sense a manifestation of your state of consciousness at the time of death—if your state of consciousness is one of wisdom and compassion, the kind of form you are going to manifest, according to Buddhist teaching, is going to be a reflection of that state.

When you are in that state of mindfulness, where your consciousness is only in the heart chakra, it is not being distracted by anything else. Then, depending on your tradition, you can employ a specific mantra,[6] which is going to create an attractive force, or force of attraction to the kind of bodhisattvic manifestation that you want to have, or to the place that you want your consciousness to end up.

In my life, I have found the Tibetan Buddhist teachings very helpful, for they provide me with a kind of "road map" to guide me through the end of my life. They help me to predict the kinds of pain, fear, confusion, loneliness, and clinging to life that may accompany me to my last moments. They help me to be able to recognize the dissolution of the physical elements of my body during the dying process and the otherwise frightening and unfamiliar visions that may come as the extremities of my body become cold, as my sense of smell and taste recede, and my hearing is all that is left until my consciousness leaves the body and begins its dreamlike journey toward its next incarnation.

In my case, I was directing my core consciousness into the heart chakra (of the central subtle-body channel) to intentionally transmit it into a spiritual realm where a compassionate, bodhisattvic reincarnation would have the best chance of being actualized. Although I don't claim to have perfected this type of *powa* practice, it was very much in the center of my consciousness as I prepared for the last moments of this life. This type of practice is taught within the Tantric[7] traditions of Tibetan Buddhism. *(For a number of different Buddhist practices, see Joan Halifax's various meditations on pages 187–206.)*

When I was younger and first encountering these practices, I thought that they were quite exotic and hard to accept. But as I have grown older and become more familiar with them—and gradually applied them to my own spiritual practice and preparation for death—they now seem very practical. And although I certainly still cling to life, I feel very lucky to be able to continue my preparations for this grand journey beyond life, and to live each day fully as if it were my last—and I am also strangely excited for a conscious death for which I am even more prepared the next time.

TINA L. STALEY Reb Zalman, you mentioned at the outset that you are over eighty, and there is a certain truth you can speak when you reach this age and are in this proximity to death; so perhaps you can tell us a little bit more about that truth?

RABBI ZALMAN SCHACHTER-SHALOMI For years I have been working with people in Spiritual Eldering seminars, and always I bring up the need for coming to terms with your mortality, without which you cannot get into "sage-ing." And that is all very nice. But then I found myself on the gurney being wheeled into the operating room, and I'll tell you—at my age—I really had to come to terms with *my dying*! You know, when you say "your mortality," it is kind of abstract; it is very different in the *kishkes*, the "guts," when you have to come to terms with "your dying"!

I have said a lot in our dialogue here about how mystical Judaism sees the afterlife, but the truth is, in dealing with people, I try to avoid a discussion of life after death until the person has come to terms with his or her mortality. Otherwise, it is almost too easy to say, "It's okay; I'll just walk out of this 'door' and enter by another." And that is not a good enough preparation; you have to go through the "needle's eye." *(See Zalman Schachter-Shalomi's "Exercises for Facing Our Mortality" on pages 161–169.)*

Those of us who have experienced a nonfatal "death" in psychedelics have experienced a coming closer and closer and closer and . . . an inevitability . . . where there is nothing else one can do but yield to death. I think when you have learned to do this in a strong way, you are much better prepared. For example, this is a practice that I used to do as a teenager when I was in *yeshivah*, studying in the seminary in Brooklyn, New York. At the time, the BMT subway trains had little booths where the conductor could sit, and I would always sit in those booths to do a little meditation while riding. Often I would imagine in a very strong and real way my impending death, saying, "By the time the train stops at Atlantic Avenue, I will be ready to give up my spirit." You see, it was a way of making my ego more and more transparent to the will of God. These kinds of practices are very important, and I feel you need to own this part of things before you explore issues of the afterlife.

I also want to say something about suffering. A lot of us are experiencing some kind of depression today. And I don't think we should take it lying down. I am referring to the social pall that has fallen on this country and the world at this time. I want to say that we should get a little angry about it; we should not yield to the depression this pall is causing. Because the world is in lousy shape, sometimes we experience even the small things as being heavy, the weight of what is happening in this world lands on top of us, and no amount of Prozac is going to handle it. So just as with our mortality, we need to own it, feel it, and decide what action directives we will take . . . including making noise about it!

DR. EDWARD W. BASTIAN You know, after going through these dying experiences and continually preparing for death, I realize that there is yet another equally profound challenge . . . that is to engage fully in daily life without fear of making commitments to others, and working for the improvement of the world, as Reb Zalman says. Preparing for death can also be a very narcissistic exercise, so I've learned that my own preparation for dying must be accompanied by a continued service to others and an enthusiastic engagement in the world (punctuated regularly by periods of silent meditative practice).

TINA L. STALEY I'm glad Reb Zalman brought up the issue of suffering, because this is most closely related to my own work, where the issue is often finding a balance between making the end of life as comfortable as possible, eliminating pain as much as possible, but also getting people to *deal with* their pain and suffering. Though, to some, this may seem contradictory. So I would like to ask Ira, how do you work with the balance between managing people's pain and helping them deal with their suffering?

DR. IRA BYOCK As a physician, I realize that I am only playing one little part in this mystery. When I meet people, I meet them bringing as much knowledge and expertise as I can to relieve their distress. Mostly it is physical distress that captures our attention in the medical field. But there is also psychosocial and spiritual distress—the sense of disintegration, the sense of loss of meaning and purpose—and I realize that I am only part of their journey through this process, and ultimately, their journey is *their journey*. If there is a larger plan here, it would seem to me that my role in this mystery is to show up, to bring what expertise I can, and to deal with things on a human-to-human level.

I acknowledge that I don't have all the answers; there may be value in suffering, but as a physician, it seems somewhat presumptuous and beyond my role to assume there is value in this person's suffering. I acknowledge that *there may be* value in it, but within my role I am going to attempt to alleviate distress. I am not a priest or a spiritual counselor, though there is overlap with those realms. So there are limitations to the role of physicians.

TESSA BIELECKI I think there is a big difference between *relieving* suffering and *escaping* from suffering. When I talked of suffering earlier, I was talking about a kind of suffering that is inevitable.

As a Christian, I believe in the value of suffering, that any suffering is potentially redemptive. Nevertheless, my whole life is dedicated to the relief of suffering, whether I have a direct contact with someone I can help, or in my prayers, putting out the intention for the relief of suffering in the universe. But there is no value in suffering for its own sake. I remember a wonderful Buddhist-Christian dialogue in which I participated. It had a very anti-Christian bias. During a question-and-answer session, someone said something like, "You Christians *wallow* in your suffering, while we Buddhists have a whole different attitude toward it." So I could have kissed the Dalai Lama who picked this question up and defended the Christian position on the value of redemptive suffering by saying, "There is only one way out of suffering, and that is through it."

However, nobody needs to go looking for suffering. Life will bring it your way whether you like or not. It is our task to relieve it wherever we see it. Sometimes we can, and sometimes we can't; suffering is a profound mystery that we cannot measure; we cannot figure out. We are not in control of it. It is another kind of dying not to be able to help someone relieve their suffering. In my monastic community,[8] we took new names as a spiritual practice. My first name was "Tessa of the Incarnation," because I am so matter oriented. After a while I added the name, "Our Mother of Sorrows." There is a great devotion to Our Mother of Sorrows in the Roman Catholic tradition. Jesus is suffering on the cross and Mary is suffering terribly at the foot of the cross, watching that suffering, and that is the greater suffering—not Jesus on the cross, but the mother at the foot of the cross. That is a terrible kind of dying.

RABBI ZALMAN SCHACHTER-SHALOMI I want to weigh in on the business of suffering. There is a difference between pain and *kvetch*, complaining. The Yiddish word "kvetch" represents that attitude that says, "I'm such a victim! *Oy!* Do I suffer." I can't imagine that kvetch has a salutary value to it; I can't imagine that it creates any inner space in one. But I know that when there is pain that is suffered, in the sense of "suffer the little children to come unto me," allowing for and creating an inner space, a sanctuary if you will, then that is very different than complaining.

But I have a question that I want to address to you, Ira and Joan: How can we prepare caregivers so that they would have an understanding of that inner process, not allowing their own anxiety to interfere with the process when they come into a room where somebody is in pain and is suffering? Often they do, and it is not helpful.

JOAN HALIFAX ROSHI   Before I take up that question, I would also like to explore the distinction, once again, between pain and suffering in Buddhism. From the Buddhist perspective, pain is a range of discomfort, physical or mental, while suffering is that story we spin around the pain.

Years ago, I was in the Solukhumbu area in Nepal with a physician at Thubten Choling Monastery. It was an overwhelming moment when three hundred monks and nuns came out of the hermitages and halls of the monastery to visit our Nomad Clinic. With me were several teenagers on a walking trip through the Himalayas, and they were stunned. There were people who had tuberculosis, leprosy, obvious cancers, many people who were in pain, but very few who were suffering. The kids just sat down and wept. I could really feel what they were feeling.

Some forms of suffering, as Zalman said, are trivial, but many forms of suffering have the potential to be transformative. In traditional cultures—Old High and indigenous cultures—there are traditional structures that induce suffering. These are called "rites of passage" and are entered into in the course of an individual's life as a way to foster maturation. Often these experiences are physically and mentally challenging. But they usually help cultivate perspective and resilience in the experiencer. *(See Joan Halifax's "Practices for Transforming Pain and Suffering" on pages 179–185.)*

TINA L. STALEY   Joan, how do you balance the Buddhist "Truth of Suffering" with the amount of suffering you are willing to "suffer" in your own life?

JOAN HALIFAX ROSHI   I think that the Buddha said that the first Noble Truth was the Truth of Suffering—and not transcendence or transformation of suffering—for a good reason. Quite frankly, I think that suffering is the only path to maturation. As Tessa pointed out, it catalyzes our capacity to mature, to develop equanimity, to develop qualities of presence in the midst of conditions, which seem untenable. Dr. Viktor Frankl[9] is an important example of this; someone who went through the worst kind of pain and suffering in the Holocaust and still found meaningfulness in his life. In the examples you and Ira gave earlier of people "living through their dying," we saw that without suffering, our life lacks depth.

Yet I like Thich Nhat Hanh's[10] phrase, "Suffering is not enough!" You don't have to look very deep to discover that you are suffering, but the problem for our own maturational process is that our suffering is rarely occurring in a context where meaningfulness can develop.

DR. IRA BYOCK You know, we can address the question on a number of different levels: there is the clinical level, the deep-psychological level, the spiritual level, and before long we get into health systems and even politics, as we already have with Reb Zalman's comment about depression. All of these are valuable ways of addressing our questions, and I am aware that in responding, we can only address one or two of these overlapping realms at a time.

Terry Tempest Williams[11] observed at the dying of her mother that it is not dying that causes suffering, it is resistance to dying that causes suffering. And so, to "die before we die," to allow us to have completed those realms of the person that we can complete, allowing us to be ready at any time to go into the Great Beyond, is a goal that I would guess many of us share.

But, Reb Zalman, I think you are right; it is essential that we prepare the caregiver adequately. For those of us who are teachers of clinicians, it is incredibly important that we teach those who would be caregivers for dying people to have some sense of comfort with their own mortality. And I worry about this—here I am going to slide into the political—I worry that hospice and palliative care, even as we have matured as a discipline, have been so focused on being accepted by the internists and the surgeons that we are beginning to look more like them than like our original selves. In the curricula of fellowship training programs for palliative care physicians, currently you find very little in the experiential realm.

I remember sitting at a breakfast meeting of directors of the fellowships in palliative medicine, and I looked at all the curriculums we were circulating, and I said, "There is nothing here about experiential requirements; are there experiential requirements in your training programs?" And one of them said, "Oh yeah, they have to do thirty visits with a hospice nurse." I said, "Yeah, I got that, but I am talking about something different. We don't allow a hospice volunteer near the bedside of a dying person until they have gone through at least thirty hours of training, most of which relates to their own issues around death anxiety, death preparedness, and they have made their own funeral plans. And yet it seems, by the looks of these curricula, that we are going to allow doctors and specialists to be at the bedsides of the dying without having worked on the basic interiority of their own issues. Because we know," and I said this to everyone at the table, "the difference between a really gifted palliative care clinician and one who is *just getting by* is not whether you can do the morphine conversion tables in your head, but whether you break eye contact when someone looks at you and says, 'Just shoot me, doc!' or 'Damn it, my life's over!' That's what matters." *(See Zalman Schachter-Shalomi's "Exercises for Facing Our Mortality" on pages 161–169 and Joan Halifax's "Meditations and Preparation for the Moment of Death" on pages 187–206.)*

Rainer Maria Rilke[12] says in his poem, "Writings from the Outside," "You be the master; make yourself fierce. Break in, then your great transforming will happen to me, and my great grief cry will happen to you." If we have not done the work of transformation for ourselves, we can't absorb that grief, and our transformation is not available for that person to grow into. So that is what worries me. I keep mentioning that we must keep palliative medicine from becoming just another specialty.

In my position, I would feel it was utterly presumptuous and frankly inappropriate for me to say that there may be value in this suffering or to inflict suffering on a patient, but as a teacher, I am in a different role. I may assign to a student, or to people in a workshop, exercises that will indeed generate some suffering as they go through them because they are already there with informed consent to grow into this experience. So exercises that may take them through a sense of discomfort, or a sense of ego dissolution, may be entirely appropriate in this context.

DR. MARILYN SCHLITZ A lot of this has to do with "change." We often talk about how we want to change, and yet, we profoundly resist change. And we are not unique in this. Other mammals do this as well. There are classic studies that were done with rats in which they could choose a low-grade electric shock at regular intervals, or no electric shock and some other penalty for them at irregular intervals, and they actually chose to have the pain if there was predictability associated with it! One of the things that the rites of passage in different cultures provide is some predictability about the process of inevitable transformation. So a culture that provides a model and a framework of predictability around death issues allows its people to begin to be able to navigate with some assurance that they understand the stages of it.

Recently, I coauthored a book called *Consciousness and Healing: Integral Approaches to Mind-Body Medicine*.[13] In this book, we are talking about embracing our own transformation, and the process by which people can *own* this issue within themselves. Ken Wilber,[14] who wrote the introduction, says it is not about the content of the "medical bag," particularly today with all the complementary and alternative approaches available. Indeed, it is sometimes bewildering for people to make sense of all of the alternatives, thinking, "Should I choose acupuncture or herbs?" But, he says, that is really not the issue. The issue has to do with the profound transformation of the holder of the "medical bag" itself, whatever the contents of that bag might be. If we can begin to do that work internally, ourselves, then the effect will begin to ripple out to others, eventually changing our cultural model.

Also, I think if we can begin to "story" together around this issue, it is going to make a difference. For we provide some predictability in our lives through story. I think if we can own the value of this conversation in our "storying" together and begin to see the transformational capacities in storying collectively, we could shift the whole future of medicine, not only in America, but throughout the world. We focus on this idea of personal and collective transformation in my newest book, *Living Deeply: The*

Art and Science of Transformation in Everyday Life, cowritten with Cassandra Vieten and Tina Amorok.[15] Here we summarize our research over ten years in which we interviewed sixty masters of the world's wisdom and spiritual traditions. In each case, it's clear that there are skills and capacities that can help us to navigate change and uncertainty.

Our educational system, as it is structured today, primarily helps us to develop from the neck up, which is to say, it helps us to develop the cognitive-rational-intellectual aspects of our being. We have privileged that in our culture. Then you look at spiritual traditions, where there are other aspects of being that get nurtured and cultivated, so that essential capacities like forgiveness, gratefulness, and love are privileged—if we could begin to build those into our educational system today, I have no doubt it would help us to live our life more naturally, so that when we do get to that final point of death, we could face it in a clearer slate, carrying less emotional baggage. And, as we learned through our research for *Living Deeply*, these are learnable skills. If we privileged them, recognizing the human being does not only live from the neck up, then we could certainly live and die *better*.

DR. IRA BYOCK And "better" means more fully, more richly, more joyously, and that too is our birthright. In some sense, the natural condition of human beings is to be joyful. That is not to say that depression and sadness are not there, but, frankly, I often see sadness and joy happening concurrently around expected death. This is remarkable and instructive. We can't change the fact that we are prone to illness, injuries, terrible suffering, and death. But we can try to leave nothing left unsaid or undone in any given day. This makes joy possible in the face of loss and impending death. *(See Zalman Schachter-Shalomi's* Giving Ourselves the Gift of Forgiveness *in "Exercises for Healing Emotional Wounds and Forgiveness" on page 173.)*

What I have learned over the years for myself has to do with apologizing more quickly. That has been a big thing for me, actually. And it works. Because if you apologize, you are offering yourself, with all of your flaws and vulnerabilities, to the other person and saying, "Will you accept me *even with* all of these flaws and failings?" And what I have found, paradoxically, is that in apologizing, and having the apology accepted, the relationship is actually stronger for my infraction than it might have been otherwise. What a remarkable thing that is; so I think there is a lot of wisdom in "Please forgive me," "I forgive you," "Thank you," and "I love you." And I say that a lot these days.

TINA L. STALEY What I am hearing is that the quality of your death depends a lot on the quality of your life. And that living fully, every day, in every aspect of your life is the best thing that you can do to prepare yourself for the end of life.

Ira mentioned earlier that palliative care practitioners should prepare themselves, should do the work themselves, so I think it is a fair question to ask, from each of your perspectives, how are you going about dealing with your own issues around death?

DR. MARILYN SCHLITZ As I have been listening and thinking about the end of life during this dialogue—and having been with a number of people as they were dying—I have realized it isn't always "the death" as much as "the leaving behind" that is so difficult. And so this idea of preparing yourself and others is important. I have a young son, and it scares me to think of leaving him alone—it scares me to the very core of my being. And yet, there are things I can do—again, working with this idea of control and predictability—to help prepare for that possibility. And I need to do it now; after all, I'm not ill, I'm in good form and have good cognitive ability, so I need to prepare the path so that at least on the material level, he is taken care of.

Carl Jung wrote, "To enjoy psychological well-being, we need a myth, story or image of death to integrate into our lived experience." And often times in our culture, there is such a fear, a taboo of dealing with these kinds of questions, such a fear of even embracing the possibility of death, let alone what happens after we die, that there's very little opportunity for us to story together some possible cosmology that could help to make the situation easier to deal with. I think that the whole question of confronting in a very conscious way the notion of death, dying, and what happens beyond that is fundamental to our health and well-being. I think about all of us in some ways as hospice workers for an old paradigm that is beginning to deconstruct under the amassing of these various data points, as midwives trying to birth something new.

In my personal cosmology of what happens after death, I embrace a fundamental interconnectedness around the cycle of life. I think the data from many disciplines of science reveals that, and spiritual traditions have been talking about this from time immemorial. I actually don't have a strong opinion about whether the personality survives bodily death. I don't have a personal conviction that it does or does not.

TINA L. STALEY Ira, how does working in palliative care help you face your own issues around death?

DR. IRA BYOCK I am aware every day as I walk through the doors of the medical center that I could be in one of those beds to-morrow. Recently we were caring for a patient (and this happens nearly every week) who was entirely well the week before; then he got a headache; then he began to lose control of one side of his body and decided to come into the emergency department, where they found tumor metastases in his brain, found the pri-mary cancer in his lung, and he is now dying—there is no cure for this man. He was entirely well as far as he knew a week before, and that could be *me* at any moment.

TINA L. STALEY That's a lesson for all of us; but those of us who do this work also know that it is a kind of preparation for dying just to be in daily, compassionate contact with those who are actually going through this, just witnessing their struggles and their courage.

DR. IRA BYOCK That's right; and doing this work is a humbling experience if you are in that mind-set. And we make mistakes too. Just a few weeks ago I was "fired" by a patient because I had—to their mind—gone "a little too far" in helping them prepare for this difficult time ahead. So it is very humbling, and you have to dust yourself off each day in order to show up again the next. It is also a chaotic environment, and yet I see it as a "temple" for my own human development. I would say the most important thing I do each day is spend time in meditation each morning. Just be-ing clear about who I am, what the world is offering me today, and then showing up with good intentions, bringing whatever skills and expertise I can to the patients and their families and the students who look to me as an example of how to behave.

I have chosen to work largely in clinical environments. And on one level I do that because I have deliberately sought a specialized training and have some skills and expertise to bring in service to fellow human beings who are dealing with difficult situations. And like Joan, I often find myself in situations that are really critical for people, whether in the emergency department or in in-patient care in the hospital settings, where people are dying . . . *often dying very hard*. I live, however, in a spiritual world. From my perspective, the world is always trying to teach me something. Always. And I show up, very aware that I am not an expert there to provide wisdom to people; I am simply there as one human being on the planet trying to be of service to another. My four rules for living are: show up, arrive with good intentions, pay attention, and don't be attached to the fruits of your labors.

TINA L. STALEY Joan, as a Buddhist and a Buddhist teacher, how are you going about dealing with your own issues around death?

JOAN HALIFAX ROSHI I think Tessa and I have a strong experience in common, because, as she said already, to live in a spiritual community is, in a way, to die a lot every day. It is really hard. You know, the mandate for people who live in spiritual communities is to unpack your ego. It is not to run a business; it is not to raise a family (in the conventional sense); it is to do your spiritual "homework." And that involves a lot of what Tessa called "the daily dying." And if you are living with ten to twenty people who are all doing their homework, let me tell you, it's a lot of work! My community spends two to four hours a day sitting in silence, meditating—they have to do that if they are going to live in the community—and if you are in a place where you have to sit down and be quiet and face your issues for four hours a day, it is going to cause your deepest issues to rise to the surface. So part of my preparation is to try to die to my ego daily for the sake of my own spiritual transformation and also for the sake of others.

I also prepare by working in situations that are generally considered hopeless. Thus, the two domains of my service are in the prison system (particularly "death row" and maximum security) and with dying people. That is where *my* rubber meets *my* road. I say, "hopeless" in the sense that if I bring any expectation into the work that I do, as a person engaged in social service, I am defeated before I even begin. In fact, just as Tessa has called herself "Our Lady of Sorrows," I have often jokingly called myself "Our Lady of Hopelessness," because, from the Buddhist perspective, hope is a real nemesis.

TINA L. STALEY How does that help you deal with your own issues around death?

JOAN HALIFAX ROSHI It develops within one a lot of resilience and a lot of love. I have to say, both in the work with dying people and in the work in the prison system, I have observed more miracles than I have in my own students. And let me tell you, when you see those sprouts breaking through the concrete of hell—in hospitals, hospices, and the prison system—something inside of you breaks open, and you can become aware of what a person is truly capable of being.

DR. EDWARD W. BASTIAN Tina, forgive me, but I can't help asking Joan a question at this point.

You know, as Buddhists, we often hear great stories of the Buddhist yogis at the time of their deaths being in meditation—we hear stories of Tibetan yogis sitting for days after they have physically died—maybe it is a romantic notion, but you get the sense as a Buddhist that the ideal death would be to be in meditation as I described earlier. But coming from a different tradition of Buddhism, Joan, I am wondering, is that part of your own life plan or aspiration?

JOAN HALIFAX ROSHI I'll confess that the greatest fear I have is that I'm going to "fail" my death, that I won't do it according to some specific standard. I really agree with Ira; everybody's death is unique. Once somebody I was working with said to me, "I don't want to be judged on how I die." And that includes me. The virtue of working with dying people and also having a practice is that it is all about the training of the mind. One Zen teacher joked, "Enlightenment is an accident, and practice makes you accident prone." It kind of hedges your bet.

As with the Tibetan yogis, there are many stories of Zen masters who went into the *yoga asana* (meditation posture) and just left the body, while leaving a death poem to their students. I feel quite open to this possibility. Of course, from the Buddhist perspective, death *is* the greatest opportunity for liberation; there is no other moment in our lives that has more potential for experiencing complete freedom than the moment of our death. Since I have witnessed on several occasions this miracle in others, as a support to a dying person, I want to live accordingly.

TINA L. STALEY Ed, in the very beginning of our dialogue, you spoke about the questions that have remained for you even after facing two near-death experiences; I'm actually thinking of your question, "What does it mean to prepare for a conscious dying process when in fact you may have no control whatsoever?" I am wondering what you think about that question now, and I would even like to broaden it, for it is difficult to imagine someone getting into some of the meditative states you have mentioned when they may be overtaken with fear. So "control" is an interesting issue here; what do think about the sense of control in the dying process now?

DR. EDWARD W. BASTIAN You know, I think that is one of the most important questions we can deal with here, and I think it also has a lot to do with "living fully," the name of our original dialogue.

Before, when I was describing the meditations I was doing on that long night in which I thought I would die, it occurred to me that there was a lot going on in those meditations; I mean, there was a lot I was doing that I didn't have to think very hard about; I wasn't doing these practices for the first time, so I could sink into them with some ease. And so I was able to overcome a lot of the fear by training. When you are totally into your one-pointed practice on emptiness, or your dissolution of the body practice, it's all happening without any analytical thought. You are into the meditation, and it is just unfolding—and this is the point—it presupposes a certain entrainment, training and habituation to these practices acquired *beforehand*. And that is why one needs to start one's practice a long time before, because it is very hard to do these things under duress or while you are in pain if you haven't done them before. *(See Joan Halifax's* The Dissolution of the Body Meditation *in "Meditations and Preparation for the Moment of Death" on page 194.)*

So, for me, this goes back to standard Buddhist—or, I should say, spiritual—practices of undermining "the false self," for in doing that, you are actually "dying dead enough," as Tessa talked about earlier. You are taking all of the steam out of the false self all of the time, and thus getting a chance to "die dead enough." And when you have made that a regular feature of your life, you are creating a situation that can "kick in" at the moment when you really need it. Because, if you haven't been dying to all those senses of the false self, as part of your practice, then all of those fears are going to pop up again around your death and overwhelm you in full force. And if you are trying to influence your next birth, and you haven't "died dead enough" to your false self, then you can expect that all of your false ideas about yourself, your fears, and neuroses are going to rise up at that time and take over, creating a less desirable rebirth.

TINA L. STALEY And what about those who are incapacitated—suffering a lingering death they cannot control—or who lose consciousness immediately because of an allergic reaction to a bee sting, like you did?

DR. EDWARD W. BASTIAN You just can't control it; all we can do is be ready, prepared through our training, prepared in every minute for it to happen. So, to the extent possible, we need to be doing our meditations, our prayers, our mantras, our mindfulness practices—we just need to be in that mindful state as much as possible so that whether it is a bee sting, a heart attack, a stroke, or Parkinson's, that state of mind will be what is underlying our consciousness. It will be so entrained in our consciousness that it will be working in the background.

TINA L. STALEY So a conscious life—*living fully,* doing the work of facing life and death, doing our spiritual work with the false self—is a kind of substitute for the conscious dying we would do in the best of all circumstances?

DR. EDWARD W. BASTIAN I don't think of it as a substitute, but rather a necessary condition for a conscious dying and, perhaps, a kind of insurance for the unforeseeable, unplanned, uncontrolled kind of death we fear.

Who knows for sure whether any of what we have said about the afterlife is true, but I think it is better for us to approach these things with a variation on "Pascal's wager." The French philosopher Blaise Pascal[16] thought it was a better "bet" to believe that God exists than not to believe, because the expected value of believing is always greater than the expected value of not believing. And I think it is a good idea to approach death and the afterlife in this way as well. It is like saving money over our lifetime so we can be solvent when we get old; we don't know that we will live that long, but it makes sense to prepare anyway. And so when we are passing out of this life, we don't know for sure, but . . .

TINA L. STALEY Again this is about living fully, isn't it? What practices from the Tibetan Buddhist tradition would you recommend to help one prepare for that moment now?

DR. EDWARD W. BASTIAN I really think one of the best preparations we have for death is the calm focusing of our minds in preparation for sleep. From Tenzin Wangyal Rinpoche[17] I have learned some of the important dream yoga techniques of the

Bon-Buddhist tradition. And from those I have learned that preparing for sleep is quite similar to preparing for death. After all, we spend a third of our life, possibly twenty-five to thirty years, asleep. Many people die in their sleep without proper preparation for death. In so doing, they lose a precious "once in a lifetime" opportunity to guide their consciousness toward a happy rebirth. Our dream-consciousness provides an important opportunity for spiritual realization. If we learn to maintain our conscious intention while dreaming, then we will also be able to keep our focus at the time of death and in the intervening period between this life and the next.

Buddhism teaches that we have an impermanent, core consciousness that endlessly transmigrates from one form of life to the next. This core consciousness is the spirit or soul; it is the essence of our being. It stores up the seeds for a future life planted in it by each word, thought, and action of a previous life. These seeds, planted in past lives, ripen in the future in the form of our bodies, minds, emotional states, intellectual capacity, and the environment in which we live. The quality of each life depends on the relative virtues of the previous life.

JOAN HALIFAX ROSHI In the Zen night chant we say:

> Life and death are of supreme importance.
> Time passes swiftly and opportunity is lost.
> Let us awaken, awaken.
> Do not squander your life.

TINA L. STALEY Tessa, is your vision of the afterlife important in your preparation for death?

TESSA BIELECKI I think so. I loved what Reb Zalman said about envisioning the afterlife appropriately, lest we get trapped in a private hell full of harps! And how we may experience the karmic results of our actions, good and bad. Part of my own simple vision, after I enter the gates and see St. Peter, includes the fifteen dogs I have lost—they are going to be the first ones to greet me! Then I imagine all the mentors and loves of my life coming to greet me, all the people who have formed me, until I get closer and closer to that intimate embrace with my Beloved. Everything I have ever gone through, everyone I have ever known, will all lead me, as it were, up to that "embrace"—a true communion of saints and animals—leading to my being reunited with my Beloved.

TINA L. STALEY And how are you going about dealing with your own issues around death?

TESSA BIELECKI As I said before, I feel that dying is "letting go of life for the sake of more life." And in this sense, we are preparing all the time. But the truth is, I haven't thought much about my physical death, because in my life, I have suffered so many psychic and spiritual deaths; I haven't had much time to think about what it's going to be like when I physically die. And that is why I value being a part of this dialogue, because it has focused me more on asking, "How do I feel about that? What do I think about that?" And I have come to realize, as I said before, that life does it for us, that all of these daily dyings that come our way are our opportunities to prepare for the big death.

The closest I have come to knowing how I would do my physical death is how I do being sick. And though I am an extremely healthy and robust person, when I am sick, I have to tell you, I have loved it! So much drops away, and all I have to do is simply *be there*. As a leader, I am multi-multitasking all the time, so just to be somewhere with a single focus is a great relief. I had a hysterectomy in 1990—the pain was terrible—but I so loved the surrender of being in a bed where all I had to do was *be* and *pray*. So when they were ready to release me, I said, "Will the insurance allow me to stay longer?" And I stayed as long as the insurance would allow! For me it was such a luxury simply to let go and surrender. And during my times of sickness, if I get the flu or a cold, my goodness, I am lying there in my bed, and it is wonderful! For years my bedroom has also been my oratory, a place of prayer. This is very important when you live a celibate life: my altar, my image of Christ, is beyond my bed where I can see him in a visual form, and the luxury of just being there with the Beloved is wonderful. So I would like to say, and I believe this rather profoundly, that I think dying will be going far more deeply and intimately into the arms of the Beloved. That is my sense of what my dying is going to be. I hope I am not being naïve; I can't be sure . . . I'll let you know!

But I also want to mention a connection with what Ed said about preparing for sleep and death being similar. Catholic Christians pray at regular times during the day. The prayers at night, called "Compline," or "completion" of the day, deal with going to sleep and compare sleep to dying. So all the prayers are about letting go. A small part of it says, "May the all-powerful Lord grant us a quiet night and a peaceful death." So we are doing that every night! And then there are prayers about being freed from the nightmares that come in sleep, which are really about the horror of dying. So every night we practice dying deeper into the embrace of the Beloved.

TINA L. STALEY "Letting go." That reminds me of a fantastic recording I heard, called *Graceful Passages*.[18] It was a compilation of contemplations on death by a variety of spiritual teachers—Ram Dass, Thich Nhat Hanh, and others. But I was particularly touched by Reb Zalman's contribution to that collection; I really felt as if you were speaking personally, and there was a peaceful sense of "letting go." Perhaps you would say a little something about that process?

RABBI ZALMAN SCHACHTER-SHALOMI It is important to practice dealing with "Into your holy hands, I commend my soul." Approaching the later years of my own life, I felt I had to do this kind of meditation myself, holding on to that feeling of serene surrender. For if you learn to do it now, you may remember it when the time comes. As the prayer says, "Be with us now and at the hour of our death." So I wanted to show people what this is like, to model it for them, so that they could adapt it as a good "rehearsal" for themselves. It goes something like this:

God . . . you made me;
From before I was born,
You took me through my life,
You supported me,
You were there with me . . .
Even when I wasn't there with You.

There were times I was sick
And you healed me;
There were times I was in despair
And you gave me hope;

There were times when I felt betrayed
And I could still turn to You;
It was a wonderful life.

I loved
And I was loved;
I sang,
I heard music,
I saw flowers,
I saw sunrises . . .
And sunsets.

Even in places when I was alone,
You, in my heart,
Helped me turn loneliness
Into precious solitude.

I look back over the panorama of my life . . .
What a wonderful privilege this was.

I still have some concerns
For people in the family,
For the world,
For the planet;
I put them in Your blessed hands.

I trust that
Whatever in the Web of Life
That needed me to be there
Is now completed.

I thank You

For taking the burden from me . . .

I thank You

For keeping me in the light . . .

As I let go,

And let go,

And let go . . .

And let go.

TINA L. STALEY Beautiful. Letting go is the choice we can make in dying. Reb Zalman, perhaps you would help us to close the dialogue with a few final words?

RABBI ZALMAN SCHACHTER-SHALOMI Earlier, I spoke of the afterlife as it is conceived in Jewish mysticism, and I tried to give it over, for the most part, without its Manischewitz wrappers, so that the deep structures of purgation would become more clear and applicable to everyone, whether Jew or Buddhist, Christian or Hindu, Muslim or Humanist. And I really believe that if you look at the teachings around how one works through the judgments, through the purgation, and get to understand what Paradise and Purgatory are *functionally,* you will begin to see that the spiritual cleaning up that we do on this side of things is really similar to what we are being taught about the purgation that happens afterward. Thus, my teacher Menachem Mendel Schneerson[19] once said after being asked about reincarnation, "Sure, we believe in reincarnation, but only a fool waits to die before he starts his next incarnation!"[20]

TEN

Are *You* Living Fully?

What is the most important thing in life? Usually when I ask people this question, they answer, "health" or "my family." But for the cancer patients I see, I have noticed that the answer changes as their time becomes more finite. In her newsletter, Carolyn Myss once said that one of the most precious commodities we have in life is *time*. When you are facing a life-threatening situation—for instance, if you have advanced cancer—you don't want to waste a minute. Every moment becomes valuable. And so, faced with a limit to your time, you begin to prioritize. You think about who you want to spend time with, where you want to spend your time, what you want to spend your time doing.

The truth is that all of us have a limited amount of time left. Most of us do a good job of ignoring this fact, at least until a doctor puts a number on it for us. Then, when we finally grasp the concept that our days are limited, we enter into a new relationship with time—*an appreciative one*—in which we treasure the time we have, and we become determined not to squander it.

Many of the families and caregivers I see, when they are talking about a loved one who is dying, say, "If only I had more time . . . " Or the dying person will say, "If I had more time, I would . . ." Whether we have hours or days or months or years or even decades yet to live, the possibility that time can be "taken away" from us makes life incredibly precious. Is it human nature to want something all the more when it is taken away from us? Do we value time so much more at the end of life because we know we are about to lose it?

It would be wonderful if each one of us could wake up every morning and remind ourselves that this day will never come again. *Every* moment of *every* day would become precious. I think that is what people mean when they talk about *quality* of life at the *end* of life—it is a savoring of life's moments, and an ability to appreciate and enjoy the exquisiteness of each day. But how do we get ourselves to do that? No one should wait to live. So how can we come face-to-face with mortality now, so as to live more fully every moment for the rest of our lives?

This is a difficult question to answer, because the answer may be very different for each of us. In my own life, strangely enough, I have always felt a kind of genetic disposition toward living and enjoying my life to its fullest. But some of this I owe to the wonderful example of my parents who taught me to participate in life and to live every moment with curiosity. That is simply who they were when I was growing up—they laughed heartily; they went out dancing; they traveled—they always seemed to be doing something interesting. I think I learned from their example so well that today my life is really that of a contemporary experientialist. Whether it is connecting to life through dancing, backpacking, art, music, or my work with cancer patients—or even trying to connect others to life through these things—this is how I am fulfilled. And yet, I can't say that my parents' example, or for that matter any natural tendency, was quite enough in itself to make this the dominant pattern of my life. There was an unavoidable amount of work to do before I could truly begin to live in this way. And I think there is an important lesson in this for all of us.

All along we have been talking about the need to face our own mortality, to face the fact of our own inevitable death, and I think this is truly the key to living fully. Once we have come to terms with that fact in a profound way, a new appreciation for life wells up in us and cannot be taken away from us very easily. But the ways in which we face "our death" may be different for all of us, and it need not be a matter of having a dreadful diagnosis or a near-death experience. For me, the opening was quite different—*it was a childhood fear of being left alone and a premonition of my own impending death.*

When I was growing up, I was left alone quite a bit. This was the shadow side of my parents' energetic lifestyle; I truly loved and admired their beautiful participation in life, but at the same time, they were unaware of just how afraid I really was as a twelve-year-old, being left alone when they were out. These nights were a personal Hell for me. During the day, I was just fine, but when the night would come, all my fears would rise up and overtake me. And throughout those years, I was constantly imagining my own death while I was alone in the house. It was very clear to me—*I could see a man on the staircase coming to kill me!* So I lived in my bedroom in fear, often shaking through the night uncontrollably because I was so terrified of that man. I pulled out my eyelashes and eyebrows and was paralyzed with fear—terrified of the night and being alone; and fearing my death, I hardly slept for years.

I lived in some version of that world of terror, and with that vision of my death, until one night many years later. I was staying at my boyfriend's loft in New York at that time. He was an artist and happened to be out that evening, and so I was all alone in the loft. I was on the phone at the time (taking care of my social worker licensing) when all of a sudden, I heard a gigantic crash! At first, I only thought, "Oh no, one of the sculptures fell!" So I went to take a look at the sculptures and found that they were all fine. I shrugged my shoulders, put on the jazz station, and turned to go back to my phone call—but then I heard something that sounded like someone walking on broken glass. I felt an icy chill go through me, and I thought, "That doesn't sound right." I then went over to the staircase where the noise was coming from and there, looking directly at me, was the very man I had envisioned my entire life! I felt myself leave my body for what seemed like an eternity as I stared at him—then I came out of it and thought, "Wake up! This is not the cleaning person; this is not somebody here working on a sculpture!" I ran to the phone and I told this poor clerk, "There is somebody breaking in!" Then I ran down to the studio, called the police, and left the building to find help.

By the time I came back there were sharpshooters everywhere, the street was full of police officers, and they had caught the burglar leaving the building. A police officer took me aside and asked, "Is this your jewelry?" I looked at it and said, "Yes." Then he said, "We think we have the guy." So they took me to identify him; I looked at him and said, "Yeah, that's him." It turns out that they had been trying for three years to catch this man. He was known as "The Greenwich Village-Soho Robber." I was told later, that after he was arrested, he kept asking, *"Who was that woman? Who was she?"* Somehow, my presence or perhaps something about how I left my body had disarmed him. It had obviously taken him out of his usual mode of operations, because he was still in the building when the police arrived! In the end, he confessed to all of the robberies and took the police to every place he had broken into. It was a wild story, and of course, people thought I was the hero, but for me, it was the moment when I faced both my worst fears and the moment of my death. I faced exactly how I thought I would die, and by facing that moment, I truly feel that I was healed.

Today, much of my work has to do with getting people to face their biggest fears—whether it is drowning, heights, commitment, or whatever—because I really feel that by facing these fears, they will be set free to live. You see, one of the curious things about our fears, especially the really big ones, is that we have the sense that we won't live through them. The truth is, we don't live *because* of them. We are paralyzed by the fear and end up avoiding the situations we are truly afraid of, living our entire lives around these fears. Really, it is less a "life" than a protracted "dying." But if we are able to face these debilitating fears—especially because we associate them with a kind of death—the effect is very much like actually facing our own death and then living to tell the story! You see, when we get in the water and face our fear of drowning, or when we take an elevator to the top of a tall building and face our fear of heights, even if it doesn't go perfectly smoothly, we find out, much to our surprise, that we lived through it! And more than that, that we had the courage, the inner strength somewhere deep inside of us, to face the terror and to grab hold of the experience! And on the other side of it—having consciously faced and lived through what we were afraid of—life is always so much sweeter. Who doesn't want that? Why should anyone wait around for some life-altering event to bring our life into focus, showing us how precious it really is? Why shouldn't we alter our own life by facing our fears now and reap the benefits for the rest of our life? I would encourage everyone who has read this book to use it as a springboard for living more fully each and every day, every minute until the last—because every moment is a precious opportunity for life, especially those that precede our dying.

TINA L. STALEY, L.C.S.W.

Duke University Medical Center, Durham, North Carolina, 2009

PART II

Resources for Living Fully and Dying Well

Introduction to Part II

THE FOLLOWING RESOURCES are for you to use for yourself or in your work with others. However, if you are to use these to help someone else, we strongly suggest that you do them first for yourself. In this way, the experience will be shared and more profound for both of you. If you are someone who believes that your loved ones did not have the kind of "good death" described in this book, or failed to do the life-review work discussed herein, you need to know that their deaths were not necessarily "failures" or "bad deaths." Each passing is highly individual, and it is not possible to judge what was a success or failure for that individual, no matter how it may have seemed to you. Nevertheless, if you have strong feelings about this, you may want to adapt some of the following resources in such a way that you can act as a kind of surrogate for another's life-completion work, doing the research and filling out the questions for them, imagining them taking the steps suggested. In this way, there may be healing around this issue for you and perhaps . . . well, we just don't know what is possible on the other side of that door . . . so why not?   — *Ed.*

ELEVEN

Life Review Exercises*

by Zalman Schachter-Shalomi

THE CYCLES OF OUR LIFE

All of us experience dramatic changes as we move through our life: from birth to childhood, from adolescence to first maturity, from middle age to elderhood, and on up to the door of death. However, grasping the larger pattern that unites these diverse stages of life often eludes us. The following practice can help us to perceive the "pattern that connects" by partitioning the continuum of our life into seven-year cycles in an attempt to discover how the parts are related to the whole.

In general, memory becomes sharper and clearer when it is associated with partitioned time. Telling someone to re-member the past in general terms usually does not yield good results; targeting a specific period of time works far better.

These exercises and practices by Zalman Schachter-Shalomi are adapted from those used in his Spiritual Eldering seminars.

When we ask someone to remember what happened during the "April" of their life, say from ages twenty-two to twenty-eight, a person may respond, "When I was twenty-eight, I bought my first home and celebrated the birth of my second child." Focusing on specific periods of time acts like a magnet in the psyche, bringing to awareness all the "filings" (the experiences) that we need to recover our past and harvest our life.

Once we have assembled the raw data of our experience, we can grasp the overarching pattern that was struggling to express itself through the ups and downs, the successes and failures that make up the rich texture of our life. Seeing which experiences remain incomplete, we can take measures to express the unlived life that beckons to us from within. Perceiving the larger pattern of our life, we can gain insight into how to harvest the rest of our life and steer it toward completion in the best possible way. Besides showing us directions for future growth, this exercise can help us cultivate an appreciation for all that we have had and enjoyed, even if our means were only modest by the world's standards. We can say, "I experienced friendship, a home and family, a useful career, and I grew in maturity over my life span." If we encountered sorrow and suffering, we can affirm, "By bearing these burdens, I grew in inner strength. I did something heroic."

1. Down the left side of a large piece of paper, list the seven-year cycles of your life: January, 0–7 years; February, 8–14; March, 15–21; April, 22–28; May, 29–35; June, 36–42; July, 43–49; August, 50–56; September, 57–63; October, 64–70; November,

	Significant moments and events	People who guided and influenced me	What this phase contributed to the continuum of my life
JANUARY (age 0–7)			
FEBRUARY (age 8–14)			
MARCH (age 15–21)			
APRIL (age 22–28)			
MAY (age 29–35)			
JUNE (age 36–42)			
JULY (age 43–49)			
AUGUST (age 50–56)			
SEPTEMBER (age 57–63)			
OCTOBER (age 64–70)			
NOVEMBER (age 71–77)			
DECEMBER (age 78–84, and beyond)			

71–77; December, 78–84 (and beyond). Use the chart on the previous page as a model to draw one of your own.

2. Across the top, divide the remainder of the paper into three columns in which you write answers to the following questions for each of the twelve periods:

   a. What were the significant moments and events of each phase of life?

   b. Who were the people who guided and influenced you during each period?

   c. What did each phase contribute to the continuum of your life?

3. To deepen your memory of people and events, you may want to devote a separate page or more to various time periods. You can enhance your memory by attaching photos to the paper, making sketches, writing little poems that evoke the era, or making a collage of newspaper and magazine clippings. Be creative in calling forth and harvesting the experiences of a lifetime.

4. Use this exercise to help recover memories of experiences that remain incomplete and that you can bring to completion as part of your "living-fully" work. You also can use the practice for working on forgiveness, recontextualizing difficult outcomes, mining the past for its untold riches, and discovering new growth.

THE TURNING POINTS

Like the preceding practice, The Turning Points helps you survey your life with panoramic vision. By revisiting some of the highlights of our personal history, we can contemplate the unfolding pattern of our life. Once we move from the past to the present with an awareness of the larger panorama, we can then look forward with a greater sense of optimism and confidence.

1. Sit in a comfortable chair or posture, relax your body, and prepare to write in your journal. Take several long, deep breaths to put yourself in a meditative state of mind.

2. Write down your memories of your . . . first holy day . . . first day in school . . . first love, first kiss . . . first and most recent experience of illness . . . high school . . . college . . . first job . . . first significant achievement . . . first failure . . . career changes . . . marriage . . . children (including births and weddings) . . . first and most recent experience with death (including your ideal departure).

3. On a piece of paper, make a time line on which you place the significant turning points of your life. Begin with your birth on the far left and fill in the experiences until you arrive at the present time.

4. Place a point beyond the present time to indicate the near future. Now ask yourself the question,

"What do I want to have done in seven days, seven weeks, seven months, or seven years?" Using your imagination, project yourself into the future and see yourself as the person who is fulfilled after having done these things.

THE JOURNEY TO OUR FUTURE SELF

For the most part, we don't know when our end will come, but whether it is days or years we must continue to look to and plan for the future. And we must continue to ask ourselves questions, whether it is how to plan for retirement, what lifestyle you should choose for the time that remains, how you want to grow intellectually and spiritually, or what the meaning of this life is. For insight into these questions, we should seek out the most reliable and knowledgeable sources, including books and professionals, but we also need to contact an inner source of wisdom to receive guidance from our spiritual Self.

In meditation we can make an appointment to visit our fully Realized Self, who can inspire us with compassionate wisdom to carry on our struggles for self-knowledge. This enlightened Self dwells beyond space and time, yet has an intimate relationship with our personality. Establishing a permanent relationship with the Realized Self can provide us with guidance for all aspects of daily life.

1. Sit quietly, close your eyes, and for a few moments follow the inhalation and exhalation of your breath as you become calm and centered.

2. Count slowly from your actual age to 120, the biblical age of accomplished wisdom. At the same time, visualize in your mind's eye walking up a set of stairs leading to the door of your Realized Self. When you knock on the door, your Realized Self, the embodiment of boundless compassion and wisdom, greets you with a warm embrace. As you gaze into your Realized Self's eyes, you feel unconditionally loved and reassured about your progress so far.

3. As a pilgrim confronting the highest, most all-embracing source of wisdom, ask your Realized Self for guidance about an issue that you have been puzzling over. The guidance that you seek can range from practical concerns ("Should I continue working at my present position or take early retirement?") to the most metaphysical inquiries ("What is the meaning of my life? Is there continuity of life after physical death?"). After posing your question, remain in a state of receptivity, allowing an answer to imprint itself in your consciousness as a sign, symbol, or an inner sense of knowing.

4. When you receive your answer, rest in the silence for a while. Then, as you look again into the eyes of your enlightened Self, receive these parting words of encouragement: "Journey on with confidence and with blessings as you proceed on your path. Visit me again whenever you need further guidance."

5. With deep gratitude, take leave of your Realized Self and with joy and confidence walk down the stairs to your point of departure. Sit quietly for a few moments, slowly open your eyes, and return to normal consciousness.

6. Record your impressions and intuitions in your journal. As you establish a long-term relationship with your Realized Self, over time you will begin to trust the guidance that comes from within and begin incorporating it in your everyday life.

TWELVE

Exercises for Facing Our Mortality*

by Zalman Schachter-Shalomi

EXAMINING OUR IDEAS ABOUT DEATH

Often we blindly accept the images of death our culture propagates without even thinking about them, most of the time seeding our body and mind with an unrealistic fear and loathing. Thus, it is important for us to unearth the sources of these images and then to reprogram our consciousness with a more balanced perspective, preparing us for a profoundly meaningful and transformative death.

1. Prepare to write in your journal by sitting down in a comfortable chair or posture, closing your eyes, and relaxing your body. Take several deep breaths, emptying your lungs completely after each inhalation.

*These exercises and practices by Zalman Schachter-Shalomi are adapted from those used in his Spiritual Eldering seminars.

Remain in a meditative state as you become quiet and centered.

2. Spend some time exploring the question, "How do I feel about death?" Is there anything to look forward to? What do you fear? In this regard, you may want to consider these questions in terms of your work in the world, family, finances, health, your emotional and intellectual life, and spirituality. Write naturally without censoring yourself, telling the truth in your own language. Remember that there are no "right" or "wrong" answers in this practice.

3. Now list negative images and impressions of death that you have internalized from our culture, from literature, films, television, advertising, religion, or your family. Be specific in describing traits and attitudes that may have influenced your attitude toward death.

4. List positive images or impressions that have influenced you. Have you acquired any traits and attitudes that are helping you to deal with this eventuality in a healthy way?

5. In your mind's eye, make a composite of the good images, impressions, and models of death and imagine what it might feel like to experience such a death in that positive context. Pay attention to your feelings and write them down in your journal.

Know that by envisioning a positive death, you are seeding consciousness and preparing it to meet that moment in a healthy way.

DOING OUR PHILOSOPHICAL HOMEWORK

In addressing the philosophical "homework," we work on synthesizing wisdom from our life experience. Contemplating the past as well as the future, we investigate the "big questions" that have occupied humanity's greatest thinkers since time immemorial with sincerity: Where do we come from? Why are we here? Where do we go after we die? What is our purpose? What is our place in the universe? To whom are we answerable? Is there inherent in life a way of being harmonious with it? In doing your philosophical homework, you confront these questions not as an interesting intellectual exercise, but as an impassioned examination of your ultimate values and commitments.

In the following practice, you will use "socialized meditation" to investigate one of the issues that humanity has wrestled with for millennia. Sitting in spiritual intimacy with a trusted friend, you will induct yourself into a state of deepened awareness and attempt to gain clarity on this major philosophical question.

1. Sit quietly with a friend who has agreed to work with you on the philosophical homework. Both of you should close your eyes for a few moments and take long, deep breaths to quiet and center yourselves.

2. When you open your eyes, your partner will pose a question to you, such as, "What do you believe

about the soul and the afterlife?" or "What is the purpose of your life?"

3. As your partner listens in silence, providing a safe, supportive field of attention for the exploration to take place, speak from your heart about this subject without censoring yourself. Explore your thoughts and feelings without trying to impress either your friend or yourself. Forget about what Socrates, Jesus, Confucius, and Mohammed have to say about this issue; speak from the immediacy and the authority of your own experience. Continue for ten minutes or so and then close your eyes and return to silence.

4. When you open your eyes, pose the same question to your partner and listen attentively as he or she wrestles with the issue. When your friend has finished, close your eyes and be silent for a few moments.

5. Now write in your journal whatever insights emerge from this session. You also might want to paint a picture, sculpt, or express your discoveries through any of the expressive arts. You also can use your insights as a launching point for further solo meditation.

SCRIPTING OUR LAST MOMENTS ON EARTH

A major task of living fully, as we have seen, involves coming to terms with our mortality. One way we can reduce our fear of dying is by rehearsing our own physical death. When we courageously confront the reality of our finitude, we convert the energy that normally goes into repressing death into an increased appreciation for the richness of our life. In the following practice, we will attempt to familiarize ourselves with the reality of physical death by envisioning our final moments on Earth. As we rehearse our deathbed scenario, we not only take steps to reduce the terror associated with death, but we enhance our capacity to experience vitality and joy in the present moment.

1. Prepare to write in your journal by getting comfortable, relaxing your body, and taking several long, deep breaths.

2. Using your imagination, experience your final moments on Earth in the most ideal manner possible:

    a. What music would you like to hear as you are dying? What poems, prayers, or sacred texts would you like recited?

    b. What would you like to taste? What scents would you like to smell? What objects would you like to have near you to touch and appreciate?

    c. What kind of physical surroundings would you like?

    d. Whom would you like to be present?

    e. Whom would you definitely not invite to celebrate your departure from the Earth?

    f. What would you like to say to those who have assembled around your deathbed? What would you like to have them say to you?

LIVING FULLY, DYING WELL

   g. How do you imagine the moment of your actual death?

   h. How would you like to have your body disposed of?

3. Record your responses in your journal. Read over what you have written several days later and then write a follow-up entry to see whether this exercise has made you more accepting and less squeamish about the reality of your physical demise.

4. As another follow-up exercise, you may want to write your own epitaph or obituary. By increasing your familiarity with the reality of physical death, exercises like these will put you on better terms with *thanatos,* the completing instinct, and facilitate the process of life harvesting.

LETTERS OF APPRECIATION

Being conscious of our own mortality, we often feel the desire to express our heartfelt appreciation to those people who have helped us on our life journey. We may have had a brief encounter with someone who changed our perspective at a crucial turning point in our youth. We may have felt uplifted by someone's wise counsel when we were going through a life-threatening illness. Or we may remember a brief but intense love affair that nourished us during a difficult transitional period in our life.

We can write letters to such people expressing our gratitude and appreciation. By writing, "How wonderful it was to have a friend like you," or "You mean a lot to me, even though we haven't communicated to each other for some time," we acknowledge our interconnectedness with the many people who have contributed to our inner richness. As the fact of death takes root in our psyche, we increasingly need to communicate what people really mean to us, how they have nourished our life, and how we have benefited from knowing them. By sending letters of appreciation to our children, spouse, close friends, relatives, neighbors, people who have generally impacted our life, and the spiritual teachers who have influenced our development, we gain closure in our relationships while widening the circle of our compassion.

Make a list of people you would like to invite to a Thanksgiving "Reunion of the Benevolent Teachers." These are the people to whom you will write letters of appreciation. In writing each letter, try to communicate the essential qualities that make the person unique and the ways in which you have grown because of your association with him or her. Don't hold yourself back: express the "mushy" sentiments that you may have avoided articulating over the years. Now is the time to open your heart and to speak with unadorned simplicity and straightforwardness. When the letters are written, you may choose to mail them or to have them mailed posthumously. (Because of unique circumstances in relationships, some people may prefer to wait until after their deaths before having their letters sent.) In either case, your actions not only will bring closure to your relationships, but will also strengthen the social web that is in danger of being fragmented and atomized by the exigencies of modern life.

A VOICE FOR THE PLANET

Coming to terms with your mortality and doing your own life-completion work brings with it a certain wisdom about life, and thus a consequent awareness of family and communal responsibility. By exercising this responsibility, you can help to heal our fractured communities and our ailing planet Earth.

1. Sit in a comfortable chair and relax body and mind by taking a few deep breaths.

2. Think back to all the animated conversations you have had with your children, relatives, friends, and colleagues in which you voiced solutions to world problems or to problems closer to home. Recall those occasions in which you spoke with such passion and clear-sighted vision that had you been a political leader, you would have inspired people to pursue an enlightened course of action on issues of local, national, or international importance.

3. Now imagine that you are addressing a parliament of world leaders. Standing at the podium, you speak fearlessly and eloquently, expressing your concerns about ecology, world hunger, the deprivation of civil liberties around the globe, religious and political intolerance, or any other issues that deeply move you. Invoking your authority as a citizen of the planet, rebuke these leaders for failing to serve the interests of the planet and the next seven generations

who may inherit a severely compromised environment and a world divided by political, economic, and religious differences.

4. Still in touch with your moral and political convictions, open your journal and consider ways in which you can express your newly discovered wisdom in the public sphere:

   a. How can you best serve the planet?
   b. How can you serve the nation?
   c. How can you serve the community?
   d. How can you be of service to your family?

5. As a further step in priming the pump of your awakened activism, you might want to write letters to your elected officials or to newspapers about issues that concern you. You also might consider joining organizations dedicated to protecting the environment, such as the Sierra Club or Friends of the Earth.

THIRTEEN

Exercises for Healing Emotional Wounds and Forgiveness*

by Zalman Schachter-Shalomi

HEALING A PAINFUL MEMORY

Life review sometimes involves reaching back into the past to repair events and relationships that caused us pain or disappointment. We can mend our personal history because time is stretchable and therefore subject to reshaping through the use of contemplative techniques. To heal the part of ourselves that is still imprisoned in the past, we can return to the scene of a questionable decision or a bruised relationship and apply the balm of our more mature consciousness. In this way, we can forgive ourselves for actions undertaken without the benefit of the more enlightened awareness we now have. By recontextualizing the past, we can release the defenses that obstruct the expression of our natural love and spontaneity and recover a sensitivity and sense of innocence that we may have lost in becoming our mature self.

*These exercises and practices by Zalman Schachter-Shalomi are adapted from those used in his Spiritual Eldering seminars.

1. Sit in a comfortable chair or posture, close your eyes, and begin breathing in a slow, rhythmic manner. With each breath, feel yourself reaching further and further into the past until you return to a time of emotional turmoil and pain. Do not resist the memory; with all your strength and awareness, make contact with your younger self who felt alone, misunderstood, unconsoled, or hurt.

2. Now let your elder self reach back with reassurance from the present and hold your anxious younger self in its arms. Visualize this embrace in your mind's eye as your mature self blesses the younger self that is smarting with pain and self-doubt about its present course of action.

3. Reaching through the fog of anxiety, the elder self says, "I come with assurance from the future. You are going to make it. You lived through this difficulty, healed from it, and learned important lessons that matured into wisdom. You acted courageously, you grew in strength and character, and in the end everything worked out well. Be at peace: even though it seems impossible now, unforeseen blessings will result from your present course of action."

4. Still feeling the embrace of your elder self, let go of the cramp around the pain. Reach into the pain, hugging, consoling, and finally sanctifying it by offering it as a sacrifice for the good of all humanity.

In this way, you elevate and ennoble that which you took to be worthless and ignoble.

5. As you let go of the burden of the past, focus your attention on your breathing and become aware of the increased energy, the buoyancy of feeling, and the sense of courage that are now available to you. Breathe in a sense of well-being and give thanks for having rescued and harvested a holy spark of your life.

6. Sit quietly for a few moments and then record your observations in your journal. Instead of writing, you may prefer to paint a picture, write a poem, play some music, or go for a meditative walk in nature.

GIVING OURSELVES THE GIFT OF FORGIVENESS

Because all of us have unhealed scar tissue from past relationships, practicing forgiveness plays a major role in our "living-fully" work. When we heal our major woundings, along with the minor bruises that accompany intimate relationships, we release feelings of anger and resentment that armor our heart with defensiveness, drain our energy, and reduce the level of our vitality. Forgiveness work has two dimensions. First, we need to take responsibility for initiating acts of forgiveness. This means overcoming our passive attitude that makes forgiveness dependent on the other person's apology. Second, we need to forgive ourselves for our contribution to the misunderstanding.

Because this kind of enlightened behavior does not come easily to us, we need to train ourselves in this noble and beneficial practice. By gaining proficiency in the art of forgiveness, we can learn how to transmute our sorrows into the capacity to love, enabling us to reach out to others with a spontaneity and openness that will add emotional richness and enjoyment to our life. As you practice the following, you will discover through firsthand experience why forgiveness is one of the greatest gifts that we can give ourselves.

1. Sit quietly and take a few deep breaths to center yourself.

2. In your mind's eye, visualize being in the presence of someone toward whom you have unresolved anger or resentment, someone who has wronged you and toward whom you harbor a grudge. As you contemplate this person's actions, consider how your lack of forgiveness keeps you chained to this relationship, drains your energy, and disturbs your emotional equilibrium.

3. Place yourself in your adversary's shoes for a moment and investigate whether your own unacknowledged needs and expectations or a misunderstanding in communication contributed to the upset or rupture in your relationship.

4. Allow your awareness to move back and forth between yourself and the other person, giving you an enlarged perspective and an objectivity with which to view the relationship.

5. Imagine that the two of you are bathed in a ray of golden sunlight that melts your resentment and allows forgiveness to take root within your heart. Rest in the warmth of this sunlight for a while.

6. With a sincere desire to mend the relationship, say, "I forgive you with all my heart and wish you nothing but unalloyed goodness. And I forgive myself for my complicity in creating this misunderstanding. May neither of us have to suffer any further painful consequences from our past encounter."

7. Now visualize being in the presence of your former antagonist and mending your relationship with kind words and gestures. As you contemplate this auspicious encounter, feel how a great weight is being lifted from you and how a sense of inner peace is replacing it.

8. Slowly open your eyes and relax for a few moments. When you return to everyday awareness, record your observations in your journal.

A TESTIMONIAL DINNER FOR SEVERE TEACHERS

This exercise uses the broad spectrum of time to reframe some hurtful relationships and situations. With this perspective, you welcome people back into your life, thanking and blessing them for the unexpected good fortune that resulted from the apparent injustice that was inflicted upon you. Besides coming to terms with these "severe teachers," we can use this exercise to investigate how our own behavior unconsciously may have contributed to our victimization. As we witness our behavior from an objective platform that was unavailable earlier in life, we can take responsibility for actions on our part that unwittingly led to personal suffering. In this way, we can end the blame game and reclaim a sense of personal empowerment.

This exercise is not perfectly suited to all of the difficult and traumatic relationships in our life, but it applies well to many of them. Keep this in mind as you do this exercise and try to take a broad, elevated perspective, seeing the karmic patterns of your life as a perfect network of connections, creating the unique person you are today. From this place, you should be able to find some way to work with most of your difficult relationships.

1. Sit in a comfortable chair or posture, relax your body, and take some long, rhythmic breaths to center your mind.

2. Divide a piece of paper into three columns. In the first column, list the guests whom you are inviting to this testimonial dinner, those who have wronged you in some significant way. In the second column, describe the apparent injustice that was inflicted on you. In the third column, describe the unforeseen benefits, the unexpected good that resulted from these actions.

3. Using the broad perspective of time, say to each of the offending parties, "I understand now that you

did me a great deal of good by your actions when you did ____, for which I want to thank you. I understand now that it was difficult for you, and it was difficult for me. But now that I forgive you, I am grateful for your contribution to my life."

4. As you consider how each of the offending parties treated you, ask yourself, "What part did I play in being victimized? Did I have an unconscious program that made me an unwitting collaborator in this scenario?" If you uncover ways in which you sabotaged yourself, extend the same courtesy to yourself that you just extended to your severe teachers. Forgive yourself. As you free yourself from the blame game and take responsibility for yourself, you can release the energy that has been tied up in resentment and redirect it into your conscious growth today.

FOURTEEN

Practices for Transforming Pain and Suffering*

by Joan Halifax

TRANSFORMING PAIN THROUGH AWARENESS

Remember why you are practicing:
To help others and yourself;
Let your heart open to this possibility.

Gently bring your attention to your breath.
Let the breath settle down and become even and regular.
Take as much time as you need in settling the breath.

Now, take your breath deep within your body.
Gently merge your awareness with your breath, as your
    body settles.

These exercises and practices by Joan Halifax are adapted from those used in her teaching and dying work, versions of which may be found on her Web site, www.upaya.org.

When you inhale, let the breath nourish you.

When you exhale, softly say the sound "ah" as though
you are sighing.

Continue this for at least ten breaths.

Gently bring your attention to your pain.

Let yourself soften to this pain.

Try to accept it without judging or fearing it.

Conscious of your pain, breathe into it.

On the out-breath, have the feeling of fully accepting
your pain.

Now, merge your breath with your pain.

Breathe into it and out from it.

Exhaling, let go into whatever you
are experiencing.

Continue this for at least ten breaths.

Now, with your mind, explore the actual sensation
of pain.

Is it sharp or dull, pulsating or penetrating?

Is it focused or does it spread out from its source?

Let yourself explore the sensation, the intensity, and the
quality of the pain.

Feel objective about your exploration, not judging or
fearing it, if possible.

Give yourself time to really explore your pain.

On the inhalation, bring warmth to your pain.

On the exhalation, soften to your pain, accepting it.

As you do this, be aware of any change in the
pain's sensation.

Do this for at least ten breaths.

Finally, gently bring your consciousness to your
    whole body.
Feel the wholeness of your body.
Rest easily with the feeling of your body.
Now, bring your awareness to your surroundings.
Accept whatever your experience might be.

When you are ready to complete the practice,
Send whatever good that has arisen out to others.

TRANSFORMING PAIN WITH AFFIRMATIONS
OF LOVING-KINDNESS

May I accept my pain with kindness.
May I be filled with compassion and loving-kindness for
    myself and others.
May the power of loving-kindness sustain me.
May love and kindness fill and heal my pain.
May I relax and send warmth and ease to my pain.
May this experience in some way be a blessing for me.
May love heal my body and mind.
May loving-kindness sustain me.

TRANSFORMING PAIN WITH AFFIRMATIONS OF COMPASSION

May my suffering show me the way to compassion.
May I freely receive others' love and compassion.
May I experience my pain with compassion.
May I be open to feel my pain.
May I be free from suffering.

May I connect with all those who have pain like I am
   experiencing; although I am in pain, so are many others.
May those with pain like mine be free of their suffering.

TRANSFORMING PAIN WITH AFFIRMATIONS OF EQUANIMITY

May I observe my pain with equanimity.

May I be present for my pain and suffering.

May I accept things as they are.

May I have the strength to face my situation.

May I accept my pain, knowing that I am not my pain,
   not my body, not my illness.

Even though I am in pain, may I handle it.

May I realize that this pain is not permanent.

May I be aware of my pain, knowing that I am not my pain.

ACCEPTANCE OF PAIN AND SURRENDERING

May I accept my pain.

May I accept this pain knowing that it does not make me
   bad or wrong.

May I be open to my pain and relax into it.

May I let go of the fear around my pain.

May I accept my pain, knowing that my heart is not
   limited by it.

May I be peaceful and let go of expectations.

May I be open with myself and others about my experience.

May this experience open me to the true nature of life.

May I accept my anger, fear, and sadness, knowing that
   they do not limit my heart.

May I be open to the true nature of life.

May I find the inner resources to be present for my pain.

May I be peaceful with this experience of pain.

May I let go of my struggle.

May I be peaceful and let go of my expectations around
my pain.

May I breathe into my pain, surrendering to it, knowing
it will change.

TRANSFORMING PAIN THROUGH THE ELEMENTS

Be conscious of your entire body and let it settle.

Accept whatever your experience might be.

Be with your body as you breathe in and out.

Your body is composed of earth, water, fire, air, and space.

Contemplate the element of earth.

Feel earth's solidity and strength.

Feel the solidity of your body and the element of earth in it.

Feel your bones, your tissue.

Your body is your home.

Feel welcomed by your body.

Invite your mind to feel at home in your body.

Contemplate the element of water.

Feel water's fluidity and power to accept anything, to purify.

Feel the water element of your body:

Blood, urine, mucus, and lymphatic fluid.

Feel the sense of flow in your body.

Feel your body's power to purify.

Let your mind settle and be pure like a still pool.
Contemplate the element of fire.
Feel fire's energy to give warmth and light, and to heal.
Feel fire's power to transform.
Feel the element of fire in your body.
Be in touch with your body's warmth and its capacity
　　to digest.
Let the element of fire open up the mind to its
　　own luminosity.

Contemplate the element of air.
Feel the power of air in your breath.
Feel the element of air in your body.
Be aware of the lightness and the strength of the
　　winds in your body.
Let the element of air bring clarity to your mind.

Contemplate the element of space, ether.
Feel the vastness of space.
Let yourself experience the openness of your
　　own nature.
Give yourself room to experience space without limits.
Let the element of space give you room for peace.

Now, bring your attention to your pain.
Let the element of earth give you tolerance for your pain.
Let the element of water absorb your pain.
Let the element of fire transform your pain.
Let the element of air release your pain.
Let the element of space give room for your pain.

AFFIRMATIONS FOR FORGIVENESS

May I know forgiveness. May the spirit of forgiveness
sustain my heart.

Forgiving Myself

May I forgive myself for mistakes made and things
left undone.

May I forgive myself for the pain I have caused myself
and others.

May I forgive myself for the pain of personalizing the
actions and words of others.

May I just forgive myself.

Asking for Forgiveness

May all those whom I have harmed forgive me.

I ask your forgiveness for hurting you.

Forgive me for not seeing who you really are.

May I be forgiven for all I have done to hurt others.

May I be forgiven for not meeting the needs and
expectations of others.

May I be forgiven for having unrealistic expectations.

May I just be forgiven.

Forgiving Others

I forgive you.

I forgive you for watering seeds of suffering in me,
whether you meant to or not.

May I freely forgive all those who have harmed me.

May I realize the spirit of forgiveness.

FIFTEEN

Meditations and Preparation for the Moment of Death*

by Joan Halifax

THE BODY SCAN MEDITATION

This practice may be done while sitting on a meditation cushion or a chair, or lying down.

Allow your body to soften into relaxation.
Bring your awareness to your breath.
Breathe deeply into your belly, allowing it to fill
    with breath.
Feel your body beginning to settle.
If you become uncomfortable at any time,
Calmly and simply adjust your posture and return to
    the meditation.

*These exercises and practices by Joan Halifax are adapted from those used in her teaching and dying work, versions of which may be found on her Web site, www.upaya.org.

Breathing deeply, bring your awareness into your body.
Allow your body to feel open and safe.
Bring your attention to the crown of your head,
And breathe into that crown, into your scalp and the top
    of your skull.
As thoughts arise, simply let them be.
Be aware of any tension in this area, and,
On your next exhalation, breathe out gratitude.

Move your awareness to your forehead,
Accepting whatever tension might be there.
Breathe into your temples;
Let them feel cool and relaxed.
Accept any tension or pain in your temples, and,
As you exhale, let your temples feel open and soft.

Lay your hands gently over your eyes as you breathe
    into them.
See if you can soften your eyes as you inhale.
As you exhale, release any hardness in and around them.
Breathe openness and awareness into your eyes
And exhale gratitude for their clarity and relaxation.

Bring awareness to the muscles in and around your ears.
Inhale fully, opening your ears.
Exhaling, feel gratitude for the ability to listen.

Inhale through your nose, feeling the air passing into
    your nostrils.
Imagine that the air you are inhaling is full of energy.

Exhale with a sense of gratitude.
Let your concentration deepen as you make yourself aware
Of where the air enters and leaves your nose.

Bring your awareness to your mouth now.
Feel your lips, gums, teeth, and tongue with it.
Let your mouth feel warm and open.
Relax the whole of your mouth, softening your jaw
    as well.
On your inhalation, smile ever so slightly.
On your exhalation, let go of any remaining tension
In your jaw, your lips, your tongue, and your throat.
Move your awareness gently through your throat
    and neck.
Let it rest lightly in this area.
Breathe into your neck and throat
And accept whatever tightness might still exist in
    this area.
Breathe out gratitude.

With your awareness in your shoulders, breathe into them,
Letting all tension melt away from them as you exhale.
Let your shoulders drop in relaxation.
Let go of any sense of weight in them, letting go of
    all burdens.
As you inhale, give your shoulders space.
As you exhale, drop your shoulders even farther.

Let your awareness flow into your arms.
Inhaling and exhaling, breathe into your arms.

Be aware of any tightness in them.
There is nothing that you need to hold on to.
With your attention resting lightly on your arms,
Breathe spaciousness into them.
Exhale relief and release.

Now touch your hands with your awareness.
Let them open—your palms facing upward.
Inhale into the palms of your hands, feeling the simple
    generosity in them.
Exhaling, imagine the tension in your arms and hands
Flowing out through your fingertips.
Let your hands feel light and alive.

Bring your awareness to your spine.
Breathe into it, letting it stretch with your inhalation.
Feel the strength of your spine in your exhalation.
As you breathe in again, be aware of your rib
    cage expanding,
And, as you exhale, feel the energy in your spine.
Appreciate the strength of your spinal column.

Now, bring your awareness to your chest and lungs.
Breathe deeply into your lungs and fill them,
So your chest rises on top of your rounding belly.
Open a space in your chest in which to breathe deeply.
Inhaling, feel your chest opening and your
    lungs expanding.
Pay attention to any tightness there, or feelings of loss
    and sorrow.

This is a very deep breath.
Breathing out, appreciate your lungs and their capacity.

Begin to breathe into your heart.
Be aware of any tightness in and around it.
Feel your heart open, trusting the intimacy of your
    awareness and breath.
Bring your attention to the tissue around your heart,
Feeling how your heart is supported by healthy tissue
    and cells.
Bring your awareness to the veins and arteries
Leading to and from your heart.
Visualize your arteries as clear and open.
See your veins carrying healthy blood into your heart.
As you breathe in, appreciate your heart and
    its workings.
Breathing out, feel gratitude for your good heart.

Bring your awareness into your diaphragm.
Let it open as you inhale deeply.
Be aware of your entire torso as you exhale and feel
    your diaphragm.
Breathing in, feel your diaphragm drop,
Giving your heart and lungs the space to expand.
On your exhalation, let go of your tension.

Let your attention flow into your liver.
Breathe into your liver and gallbladder.
Be aware of any tightness you may have there.
As you inhale, give your liver and gallbladder space.

As you exhale, let go of any feeling of anger that you
might be holding.
Breathing in and out, appreciate your liver and gallbladder.

Now bring your attention into your stomach.
Breathing in, be aware of the digestive function of
the stomach.
Breathing out, let yourself feel gratitude for the
functioning of your stomach.

On your next inhalation, let your awareness flow into
your kidneys and lower back.
On your exhalation, be aware of any anxiety you may
be experiencing.
Now breathe strength and awareness into your kidneys
and lower back,
And exhale, giving the gift of spaciousness to them.

Bring your awareness to your bowels and bladder.
As you inhale, feel your gut expanding with the inhalation.
As you exhale, be aware of any tension in your bowels
and bladder.
Remember the function of elimination performed by
your bowels and bladder.
Bring breath and space to your bowels and bladder.
Feel grateful for your bowels and bladder.

Now, move your awareness to your genitals.
As you inhale, be aware of how your genitals feel.
As you exhale, give these feelings space.

Breathing in, appreciate your genitals.
Exhaling, give your entire pelvic area a feeling of space
and ease.

Bring your attention to your thighs.
Breathe into them as you settle your attention there.
Breathing out, let your thighs relax and soften.
On your inhalation, be aware of the strength of
your thighs.
Breathing out, appreciate the support of them.

Move your awareness to your knees.
Breathe awareness into them.
On the exhalation, be aware of the small muscles around
your knees.
Feel grateful for your knees,
And breathe healing into them.
Let go of any tension and pain in your knees as you
breathe out.

Bring your attention to your calves and shins,
And breathe into your calves and shins.
Exhaling, be aware of any tension in them.
Breathe in spaciousness to your calves and shins,
And exhale gratitude that your legs have taken you
this far.

Now, breathe into your feet,
Bringing all your attention to their flesh, muscles, toes,
and soles.

On your out-breath, be aware of any tension in them.
On your in-breath, imagine that you are breathing
All the way through your body and into your feet.
On your out-breath, appreciate your feet from their soles.

To complete this practice—slowly, gently, smoothly—
Bring your awareness from the soles of your feet to
     your legs,
To your pelvic area, to your stomach and liver,
To your chest, heart, and lungs,
To your spine, to your shoulders, arms, and hands,
To your neck, to your face, to the top of your head.
Inhale and exhale smoothly as your awareness travels up
     through your body.
When you have reached the top of your head,
Return your awareness to your breath,
Then let it gently spread to the whole of your body.
Stay in this awareness for a while.

Take a few moments to relax with an open and
     quiet mind.
Send your sense of well-being to others on your breath,
And, when you are ready, open your eyes.

THE DISSOLUTION OF THE BODY MEDITATION

One of the highest disciplines of spiritual practice seeks to transform the experience of dying, death, and rebirth into the experience of enlightenment and liberation. The practice that follows models the experience of active dying and death and has been used as a way for spiritual practitioners to gain control over the dying experience, thus transcending death.

According to tradition, when the bases of our consciousness begin to collapse, we are in the process of dying and are soon to meet death itself. These bases of consciousness are sometimes referred to as "winds" that control all forms of motion in the body, including talking, swallowing, spitting, urinating, defecating, movement of the joints and limbs, movement of the eyes, movement of the blood vessels, respiration, and digestion.

As we near death, the winds that have served as the bases for our consciousness, or of our moving life force, merge into the right and left channels on either side of the central channel, which runs from the crown of our head to the base of our spine. The winds then dissolve into the central channel and, as a result, loosen the constriction around our heart center, thus liberating the more subtle aspects of the mind.

When the winds begin to transform in the process of dying, the mind goes through radical shifts. Most experience the transformation of the winds as an annihilation experience, but an advanced spiritual practitioner actually "practices" in order to have this type of experience and, in this way, gains control of the mental states that arise in the process of dying. This is done so that death can be experienced as the liberation it truly is.

The description and practice of the dissolution of the elements in the experience of dying arose over many centuries from the finely tuned observations of skilled meditators. Although it is an esoteric spiritual practice, it nevertheless confirms the observations of countless caregivers who have observed similar physical, mental, and energetic changes occurring in those who are dying. It also has been an aid, a map, and a source of inspiration to those who are actually going through or preparing to go through the experience of dying.

This description of the dissolution of the elements also includes the dissolution of the aspects of our subjective experience that give us a sense of an identity. These five aspects include the experience of our body, our feelings, perceptions, mental formations, and the capacity to discern. These five aspects are also affected in our experience of sickness and aging. When we have been ill, for example, we can feel the body's heaviness and weakness; and we can experience some of the signs and symptoms described in the dissolution process. As we age, the force of gravity becomes more and more apparent to us as our physical strength diminishes. Our senses become less sensitive and our grasp of the world lessens. In both sickness and aging, we are given a taste of what we will face as we are dying.

Posture

Take a comfortable posture and allow yourself to adjust your position as needed through the course of this practice. The top of your head, the fontanel, is directed toward the visualized image of your choice, any being who represents to you the essence of awakening, of compassion, of love, of essential goodness. Your hope is that your consciousness, when it leaves your body, will leave through the top of your head and will manifest as the essence of enlightenment.

The Mind

Allow the mind to become still.
Let the breath become even and smooth.
Focus your attention on your breath.

As always in this kind of practice, whatever arises—
Resistance or concern, grief or joy, boredom or story—
Simply notice it, accept it, and then return to the breath.
Concentrate on your breath and let your body relax.
Although this may put you at the edge of sleep, do not
    fall asleep.

All beings, in one way or another, are dying.
Although some of us are closer to death than others,
The time of our death is always uncertain.
If you are not actively dying at this time,
Imagine yourself as dying, and remember,
On some level—you are.

You may have a sense of who you are as an identity,
But you are now going to release that identity
Into spaciousness, into vastness.
Let yourself attend to your breath.
Be in the breathing.
Mark the out-breath with a slight increase of attention,
An increase of commitment to the breath of releasing,
    expiring, letting go.

Imagine that this is an actual description of your dying.
Notice what arises in you as you do this practice.
Let each of the feelings and sensations come up for you,
Pass through your mind and body, be noticed, and
    then released.
This practice is about awakening to your
    essential spaciousness.

The Dissolution of Earth into Water and the Unbinding of the Body

Imagine that you are lying in your bed at home.
You are dying.
Friends and family are around you,
But you are barely aware of them.
You are somewhat agitated, but you accept this state
 of mind.

Your body is thin and weak.
You cannot sit up or even lift anything.
You do not have, nor do you need,
The energy to do anything but simply be here.
You are releasing this flesh and bone, this nerve
 and marrow.

You are letting go of it all as you die.
Feel your body becoming heavy, pressed down by a
 great weight.
This is a heaviness that is dense and deep, going right
 into the core of your body.

Let yourself be pressed down by the weight of death.
As you become weaker, your body feels less defined.
Your arms and legs feel as if they are not quite a part of you.
It seems as if your legs could slip off of your hip bones,
Your arms could slip off your shoulders.

Experience the body dissolving, melting.
There is no distinction between the bed and you.

It's as if you were sinking into water.
And with this sinking feeling
Comes a sense of even greater weakness and tiredness.

The boundary between your body and space is
    beginning to dissolve.
Wake up as the body begins to let go.
Your senses are less attuned to the outside world.
Your sight is dim and dark.
It is difficult to open and close your eyes now.
Your sensory grasp on the world is loosening.
The outside world is slipping away from you.

Your skin pales as your blood pressure drops.
The blood withdraws into the center of your body.
There is no strength left now in what was this strong body.
You are drowsy and weak and have no interest in the
    outside world.
You sink deeper and deeper into an undifferentiated
    mental state.
Whatever visions you see appear like shimmering
    blue mirages.
This is the dissolution of body and of our relationship to
    the physical world—
These feelings of heaviness, drowsiness, being
    weighed down,
The loss of definition, the withdrawal of color from
    our body,
The loss of control, and our inability to see the form
    world around us.

In this state of mind and body, be awake, be present
without effort.
The mind can be still and reflective as you wake up, as
you let go.
Be present as this body is dying.
This body is not you.
This is the dissolution of the element of earth
As it sinks into water, and form unbinds into feelings.

The Dissolution of the Water Element into Fire and the Unbinding of Feelings

Feel your body dissolving.
As you are letting go, your hearing is diminished,
And you sink into an undifferentiated state of mind.
You have now lost control of the fluids in your body.
Your nose is running; saliva may be leaking out of
your mouth.
There is a watery discharge coming out of your eyes.
It is difficult for you to hold your urine.
Your generative fluids have dried up,
And your skin is clammy.

As fluids leave the body, the body becomes parched.
Your skin is papery.
Your mouth is drawn, and your lips are chapped.
Your tongue is thick, sticky, and heavy.
Your throat is scratchy and clogged.
Your nostrils seem to cave in, burning with dryness as
you inhale.
Your eyes feel sandy and sting.

You are not passing much urine.

You have a thirst that no amount of water can quench.

Moisture is leaving your body, never to return.

Wake up as you are desiccating.

Let go into this dryness.

Release the fluid element of your body, the element of
water and of feeling.

You have ceased to experience pain, pleasure, or
even indifference.

You do not have feelings related to happiness
or unhappiness.

You are numb and do not differentiate between physical
and mental impressions.

Those kinds of distinctions are not important to you now.

When you look behind your eyes, you see a vision of
swirling smoke.

See this haziness that dissolves all differences.

The water element is dissolving into fire.

This is the end of your responsiveness to phenomena.

As you let go, wake up in this vision of swirling smoke.

The Dissolution of the Fire Element into Air
and the Unbinding of Perceptions

As the fire element of your body begins to dissolve into
air, your body feels cool.

Heat withdraws from your feet and hands into the
body's core.

Your breath is cold as it passes through your mouth
    and nose.
Your mouth, nose, and eyes dry out even more.
Your ability to perceive is further diminished.
The fire element is dissolving into the element of air.

You cannot smell anything.
You are not hungry, nor can you digest food.
You cannot drink or swallow.
The in-breath is less strong now, and the out-breath
    is longer.
Your mental perception alternates between lucidity
    and confusion.

You cannot see, hear, taste, touch, or smell as the sense
    fields fade away.
Your in-breath is short.
Your out-breath is long.

You cannot remember the names of your loved ones,
And you cannot recognize those around you.
You have lost any sense of purpose in your life,
And have no interest in what is going on around you.
You may feel as if you are being consumed in a blaze of
    fire that rises into space.
Let go into this fire and see it as your mind
    releasing itself.
Or you may see a vision of sparks, almost like fireflies.
Wake up in this vision of shimmering sparks behind
    your eyes.

Let yourself discern the truth of dying.

This is the dissolution of the fire element into air and the
unbinding of your ability to perceive.

The Dissolution of the Wind Element into Space
and the Unbinding of Mental Formations

You now have given up any sense of volition.

There is nowhere to go, nothing to do.

Accept this aimlessness, free of meaning and purpose.

You are at last free of these pressures.

Your in-breath is short; your out-breath is long.

The mind is no longer aware of the outside world.

As the element of air is dissolved, you are having visions.

Your visions may be jewel-like and filled with insight
that can never be expressed.

These visions relate to who you are and how you have
lived your life.

You may be seeing your family or your ancestors in a
peaceful setting.

You may be seeing beautiful people, saints, or friends
welcoming you.

You may be reliving pleasant experiences from your past.

Or you may have demonic and hellish visions.

If you have hurt others, those whom you have injured
may appear to you.

Difficult and dreadful moments of your life may arise to
haunt you.

You may see people with whom you have had negative
interactions attacking you.

You may even cry out in fear.
Do not identify with these visions.
Simply let them be.

The element of air is dissolving.
You do not have to do anything.
Just practice this breath of release and let go
    of everything.
Your tongue is thick and heavy; its root is blue.
You have lost your taste for life with the sense of taste.
You cannot feel texture or body sensations.
Your body is barely moving.
The last energy of your body is withdrawing now to
    your body's core.
Whatever heat is left in your body now resides in the
    area of the heart.

The in-breath is short, a mere sip of air.
The out-breath is long and uneven.
Your eyes, gazing into emptiness, roll upward.
No intellect is present.
Your consciousness at this point is reduced to a smaller
    and smaller entity.

Three rounds of respiration.
Your body lifts slightly to meet the breath, which does
    not enter.
Your mental functions cease altogether.
Your consciousness has dissolved into space.
The perception from the outside is that you are dead.

Breathing has stopped.
Brain functioning has stopped.
The body feels no sensation.
Know this empty state.
Know this stillness and surrender to it.
Experience it.
This is the element of wind dissolving into space.
Become space.

At the moment of physical death, one sees the small,
   flickering flame like a candle.
Now it is suddenly extinguished, and you are without
   any awareness.

The Inner Dissolutions

From the crown a white drop
Is propelled by the inner winds
Downward through the central channel toward the heart.
This is the masculine essence, and anger transforms into
   profound clarity.
You experience an immaculate autumn sky filled with
   brilliant sunlight.

A red drop from the base of the spine
Is propelled upward through the central channel toward
   the heart.
This is the feminine essence, and desire transforms into
   profound bliss.
You experience a vast and clear copper-red autumn sky
   of dusk.

The white and red drops meet in the heart and surround
    your consciousness.

The winds enter your consciousness.
You are now freed from the conceptual mind.
Thick darkness like a deep autumn night sky appears.
You dissolve into unconsciousness.
Out of this nothingness, luminescence arises.
You are one with a clear dawn sky free of sunlight,
    moonlight, and darkness.

You are bliss and clarity.
Now, the Clear Light of Presence is liberated,
The Mother Light of your awareness.
This is your ultimate Great Perfection.
This is the actual moment of death.[1]

SIXTEEN

Practices for the Caregiver and the Bereaved*

by Joan Halifax

PRACTICING WITH A DYING PERSON

This practice involves a simplified version of the Body Scan Meditation, a shared breathing practice with an emphasis on the exhalation and a guided visualization on the light. The practice is supported by an assistant who makes sure that there are no interruptions, a caregiver who guides the dying person, and the dying person. It can be done in the hospital or at home, but the most important element in the practice is the relationship of trust between the dying person and the caregiver.

The Practice

The caregiver and an assistant make certain that the atmosphere around the dying person is comfortable and quiet. The assistant is

---

These exercises and practices by Joan Halifax are adapted from those used in her teaching and dying work, versions of which may be found on her Web site, www.upaya.org.

there to make sure there are no interruptions and to get the dying person whatever he or she may need. The caregiver helps the dying person find a position that he or she will be comfortable in for up to an hour.

The practice is explained to the dying person. For instance, "This is a way that we can meditate together. It involves several relaxation exercises and a guided visualization. Try to let go into what we are doing. I really hope this will help to bring you some peace." The practice is calibrated to the situation and, above all, to the needs of the dying person. The lights should be low and the dying person covered up so he or she is comfortable.

The caregiver then does a simple version of the Body Scan Meditation with the dying person, beginning with the feet. This is the relaxation exercise. The caregiver might say, "Let the feet and toes relax," and so forth, and then move on up to the top of the head, and then back down through the body to the feet. The caregiver then invites the dying person to relax his or her entire body and mind.

When the dying person is ready, the caregiver breathes gently with the dying person. When the caregiver feels it is appropriate, he or she quietly (though still audibly) breathes the phoneme "ah" with the exhalation of the dying person. The caregiver does this for five to ten minutes, so the one who is dying can really bring his or her attention to the exhalation. If the dying person wishes, he or she may also say "ah" on the exhalation. The sound "ah" is soft, almost like a yawn. The feeling is of surrender, of letting go.

When the dying person has settled into deep relaxation, the caregiver softly suggests that there be a short period of silence. The caregiver may then say an appropriate prayer favored by the dying person or give a guided visualization on light. For example, the caregiver might suggest that the dying person visualize a boundless ocean of light, then guide the dying person to merge with or dissolve into that luminosity.

The session can finish with a dedication, a deep thanks, or a period of silent meditation. Sometimes it is helpful for the caregiver to ask the dying person how he or she felt about the experience.[1]

GIVING AND RECEIVING: A PRACTICE OF MERCY

The practice of giving and receiving is done to develop our compassion and our ability to be present for our own suffering and the suffering of others. In teaching this practice for more than twenty-five years, I have been told again and again that this one practice has helped many people immeasurably in attending to their own fears around pain, suffering, dying, and loss and has given them a real basis for the joining of compassion and equanimity.

Giving and Receiving

To begin, sit in a meditation posture, relax in a chair, or just lie down.

Close your eyes and allow your body and mind to settle, relaxed and open.

You can say this prayer, or the prayer of your choice.

To create a sense of openness in which the giving and receiving can take place, say:

Recognizing the utter futility of my selfishness
And the great benefit of loving others,
May I bring all beings to joy.
May I send all my virtues and happiness

To others through the strength of my practice,
And may I receive the suffering, obstacles,
    and defilements
Of all motherly beings in all realms.

Begin by inhaling whatever you are feeling,
Whether fear, agitation, anger, or resistance,
And simply, humbly accept it.
On the exhalation, breathe out well-being.
Clear your mind by bringing awareness to what is
    agitating you,
Breathing it in and accepting it with loving-kindness.
Then, as you exhale, give yourself space.
Do this breath practice until you are calm and alert.

Working with the Texture of the Breath

When you are settled, begin the second stage of
    the practice,
Establishing a rhythm of breathing.
On your inhalation, imagine that you are inhaling heavy,
    hot air.
On your exhalation, visualize yourself exhaling cool,
    light air.
Continue with this pattern for a while,
Breathing in heaviness and breathing out lightness
Until it is familiar to you.
The heaviness is suffering; the lightness is well-being.

Now, imagine that you are breathing through all the
    pores of your body.

On the inhalation, heavy, hot air enters through every pore.
On the exhalation, cool light flows from every pore.

Dissolving the Metal Sheath Around the Heart

Now, visualize a metal sheath around your heart.
This sheath is everything about you that is difficult
    to accept:
Your self-importance, selfishness, self-cherishing, self-pity;
It is the band of fear that hardens your heart.
This practice invites you to dissolve this metal sheath
And open your heart to its natural nonjudgmental state
Of warmth, kindness, and openness.
You can do this by visualizing the metal sheath
    breaking apart
When the inhalation of suffering touches it.
When the heart opens, the hot, heavy air vanishes into
    the vastness of space.
What arises is a natural mercy.
It is this quality of unarmored, vulnerable heart that
    allows you to be with suffering
And at the same time to see beneath the suffering.

Awakening the Heart

Bring to your awareness someone, dead or alive, with
    whom you feel a deep connection:
A parent, child, pet, your grandmother, your dearest
    friend, a beloved teacher;
Preferably, someone who is (or was) suffering.
You would do anything to help them.
Be with them now and feel what they are experiencing.

Let your whole being turn toward their suffering
And your wish that the suffering might be relieved.
Can you see how vulnerable they are?
Like a mother who will do anything to help her child,
You will do anything to help your beloved.
Visualize the suffering of your beloved as polluted,
   hot smoke
And breathe it in through your whole body.
The instant that the inhalation of suffering touches
The metal sheath of self-centeredness around your heart,
The sheath breaks apart, and your heart opens to
   the suffering.
The hot smoke instantly vanishes into the great space of
   your heart,
And from this space spontaneously arises an exhalation of
   mercy and healing.
Send a deep, cool, light, and spacious healing breath to
   your beloved.
Let the out-breath flow through every pore of your body.
Let this one's suffering remind you of the many others
Who find themselves suffering in the same way.
This person is your connection to all of them.
Breathe in their suffering
And let your heart break open.
Send them healing with your out-breath.
Continue with this practice.

Practicing with Your Own Situation

Now, bring the practice to your own life.
Remember a time when you were in a difficult situation.

You may still be holding the energy around this difficulty.
You may have been hurt, angry, depressed, outraged,
    or afraid.
Remembering the feeling as vividly as possible,
Breathe it in as hot, heavy, polluted smoke.
Let go of any sense of blame, and any object of blame.
Inhale the raw feelings directly as the hot smoke
    of suffering.
Take it in completely through every pore of your body.
Own the heat and rawness of it completely.
This practice takes a lot of courage;
You might find yourself resisting the inhalation
    of suffering.
If so, you can breathe in your resistance as hot,
    heavy smoke.
You can breathe in alienation, pity, boredom, arrogance,
    confusion, grief, or clinging—
Whatever flavor your suffering of the moment takes.
Let the metal ego sheath dissolve to reveal the vastness of
    your heart.
Exhale the sense of openness, loving-kindness, and
    surrender that arises.
Shower these qualities on yourself in a rain of cool,
    healing light.

Don't analyze what you are doing.
Don't try to figure it out.
Don't justify it.
Simply inhale the heavy, hot smoke of your suffering
And exhale sympathetic space.

As you breathe in your hot, heavy, tar-like suffering,
own it completely.
Then breathe out clarity and surrender, relief
and kindness.

Connecting with Those Suffering as You Are

Now, consider that at this very moment many others
are experiencing
The same kind of misery as you—anger or anxiety,
for example.
The details of their distress are not important.
The point is to connect with the truth that others are
suffering just as you.
Feeling your distress and theirs, inhale it for others as well
as for yourself.
This will not increase your own suffering;
It will open your heart to the truth that others are
suffering as you are.
It will give you the opportunity to connect with them.
Let this connectedness open your sympathy toward
yourself and them.
And as you breathe out clarity and kindness,
Let the breath go to all those who are suffering as you are.

Now dissolve this visualization and continue with
the practice,
Breathing in universal suffering, yours and that of all
beings, as heavy, hot smoke.
The hardness around your heart dissolves and your great
heart appears

As the smoke of suffering vanishes into its vast space.
Through every pore of your body, breathe out goodness
and healing
As a cool, light breath.

Practicing with a Parent

Bring into your awareness a parent or parental figure
With whom you have had the greatest difficulty.
Keep the rhythm of the hot, smoky in-breath and the
cool, light out-breath,
Consider how this one and you have suffered.
For a moment, imagine gazing into the eyes of
your parent.
Looking at her or him in a mental photograph might help.
Notice if this is difficult for you.
See the wear on her or his face.
Maybe her or his life has been full of disappointment
and frustration.
Maybe she or he was afraid.
Maybe she or he was numb.
See if you can allow yourself to be in touch
With the difficulties that this one has had.
Imagine how things might have been different for her
or him.
Imagine how she or he could have given you love in a
form that nourished you.

Imagine your parent as a three- or four-year-old child.
Perhaps you remember a photograph of her or his face at
this age.

See her or his face free from weariness.
Imagine this one without suffering.
If it is difficult for you to see your parent in this way,
Please notice the resistance that might be there.
This is all right.
Inhale the resistance; exhale acceptance and open space.

In practicing this way, perhaps you experience anger,
 disappointment, or heartbreak.
Simply allow yourself to feel whatever arises.
Breathe deeply into your belly and resolve to transform
 your alienation
In order to help others and to help yourself be free
 from suffering.
Inhale your own suffering as heavy, polluted, hot smoke.
The instant that the in-breath of suffering touches the
 metal sheath
Of self-centeredness around your heart,
The sheath dissolves, and your heart can open to your
 own suffering.
The hot smoke of suffering instantly vanishes in the
 presence of your heart,
And from this space an exhalation of mercy arises
 spontaneously.
Send a deep, cool, and healing breath to yourself.
Let this out-breath flow through every pore in your body.

Now, reconsider the parent whom you have visualized.
You have seen this one as a child.
Now see her or him as you last remember her or him.

Breathing in the hot, heavy smoke of her or his suffering,
Let it dissolve the hardness around your heart
So that your great heart can absorb and
    transform suffering.
On your exhalation, send all your strength,
Understanding, caring, and love to your parent.

Allow yourself to let go of the visualization of
    your parent
And keep the rhythm of the breathing steady,
Breathing in hot, heavy smoke,
Smoke that dissolves completely into the vastness of
    your heart.
Breathe out through every pore of your body coolness
    and healing.
Send it to the whole world.

Practicing with a Dying Person

Imagine that you are sitting with someone who is dying.
See her or him as clearly as you can.
You are sitting quietly and peacefully next to her or him,
    following her or his breath.
You see that she or he is in pain.
You can almost feel that pain.
Visualize the sheath of fear around your heart,
That tough membrane that you use to protect yourself
    from the world.
Inhale her or his pain as hot, heavy, grimy smoke.
Breathe in through every pore in your body.
Let your heart break open to her or his pain.

Now, release the pain completely as you exhale a breath
    of loving-kindness,
Giving her or him all the good that you have known in
    your life.

Practicing with Your Own Experience of Dying

Now, imagine that this one who is dying is you.
See yourself on your deathbed.
Your body feels tired and heavy.
You might be fearful.
Inhale that fear as heavy smoke.
Let it dissolve the tightness around your heart.
Feel your heart open to its natural greatness.
Then let go of your breath completely
As you send all the good in your heart to the world.

Imagine that this is the moment of your death.
Let your heart completely relax and open like a flower
As you let go of your last breath,
Giving the merit of your life to beings everywhere.

Now dissolve the visualization
And rest your body and mind in openness.
Then send whatever good
You might have derived from the practice
To suffering beings everywhere.

Practicing Giving and Receiving with Another

After practicing giving and receiving with yourself,
Turn silently toward someone close to you.

Stay with the practice, letting yourself inhale
    universal suffering.
The metal sheath around the heart breaks open,
And the smoke of suffering dissolves into the vastness of
    your heart.
Through every pore in your body,
Exhale all of your goodness and healing for the world.

Gaze at the chest area of the one sitting across from you.
If you wish, you may gently synchronize your breathing
    with each other.
Practicing nondual presence and continuing the practice
    with your inhalation,
Inhale hot, heavy smoke, letting that smoke dissolve the
    sheath around your heart,
And exhale a cool light breath.

If fear or resistance comes up, just notice it.
Remember the depth of your commitment.
Rekindle your determination if fear makes if difficult
For you to practice directly with another.
Breathe in the fear and breathe out ease.
When you are ready, let your eyes rise
To gaze into the throat area of the person across
    from you.
Continue sending and receiving.
Let the specific identity of this one sitting across
    from you
Become a little more revealed to you.
Stay in the truth of your practice.

When you are ready,
Let your eyes rise to meet the eyes of the friend sitting
    across from you.
Simply being present, gaze into the eyes of your friend.
Let your good heart connect with this one sitting across
    from you.
This one, like you, has suffered.
This one's life, like all lives, has had its share of pain
    and sorrow.
This one, like you, will die one day.

See the lines of weariness, concern, disappointment, or
    sadness in this one's face.
It is not necessary to give what you see a story.
In a general way, just be with the life that this one has lived.
Keep it very simple.
If you feel as though you are beginning to fixate,
Close your eyes and return to your breathing practice
And open your eyes when you are steady.

Now, imagine this one as a three-year-old child.
See her or him as she or he might have been when
She or he was very young and free of any pain.
Imagine that this young, fresh, and hopeful being is still
    alive in your friend.

Now, in your imagination, bring your friend into
    the present.
Through innumerable lifetimes, all beings, whether
    male or female,

Have been our mother in one lifetime or another,
Have given birth to us, carried us into life,
Have cared for us, have nurtured us, have protected us.
Allow this one to be your mother,
And see not only her difficulties, but also her compassion.
Your gratitude to her is very deep.
With all your heart, you want to repay her kindness.

This one has also been your child.
See not only the mother in her or him, but also
     the child, your child.
Imagine the love that you might feel for your child.
You would do anything to help this one be peaceful
     and free of distress.

On your next inhalation, breathe in the suffering of
     this one.
Breathe in dark, heavy, hot smoke that breaks apart
The metal sheath of self-importance around your heart.
The smoke of this friend's suffering dissipates into the
     vastness of your true heart.
On your out-breath, exhale a cool, light breath of kindness.

Remember, this one with whom you are practicing
     will die.
We do not know when or how.
See how her or his life is hanging by a breath.
You hope that this one will be able to come home to her
     or his own true nature.
Your heart of compassion is wide open.

Put any negative aspects of your personality into the
    metal sheath around your heart.
On your next inhalation, the dark, heavy, hot smoke
Of this friend's suffering transforms your negativity
    into mercy.

Now, imagine that this one sitting across from you will
    not be alive tomorrow.
There is always that possibility.
The thought of impermanence can help deepen the
    commitment to the practice.
Breathe in suffering. Breathe out kindness.
When you feel ready, allow your eyes to close.
Let go of this friend sitting across from you.
Open the focus of your practice to the universe.
Inhale universal suffering, dissolving your own
    self-importance.
On your out-breath, give away all of your goodness to all
    beings who suffer.

PREPARING THE BODY AFTER DEATH

Methods of caring for the body after death vary from culture to
culture. What follows are some suggestions that come from my
experience as a Buddhist and a caregiver of dying people.

Immediately after Death

Keep the atmosphere around the deceased simple and peaceful.
If possible, do not disturb or touch the body immediately after
death. If the body must be touched, do so very gently.

Pray for peace and freedom for the one who has died. If appropriate, read sacred texts or conduct any practices or death rituals from the deceased's tradition.

Before the Onset of Rigor Mortis

As rigor mortis takes about two hours to set in, you will have enough time to bathe and dress the body. This can be done by family members or friends as a last act of intimacy and respect. Know that before and at the time of death, the dying person may have defecated, urinated, vomited, or sweated. You may want to give the body a sponge bath with a mixture of aromatic herbs (such as yogi tea) and a small amount of alcohol to close the pores. Place cotton in the rectum so that wastes do not leak from the body, and a condom or rubber glove on the penis or cotton in the vagina. The teeth and mouth can be cleaned. Do not remove dentures or you may not be able to put them back in after rigor mortis sets in. Reflexive muscle spasms will occasionally occur in the limbs or facial muscles.

Mindfully dress and arrange the body before it stiffens. Dress the person in light clothing, and do not cover the body with bedding. The body needs to stay as cool as possible. A fan, air conditioning, or an open window can be helpful in keeping the body fresh.

Often the eyes are open after death. If you wish, you can gently close the lids and tape them shut. The mouth might be open. You can close it with a scarf tied around the head. The last place in the body that warmth will leave is the heart area. If the heart is still emanating warmth, be particularly mindful of what is happening in the environment of the deceased. The Buddhist tradition tells us that such warmth usually occurs in those who have some quality of realization at the time of death.

What to Do with the Body

Although you might be concerned that it is unhealthy to keep a body in the house after death, there is nothing inherently dangerous about doing so. Treat a dead body in the same way you would a living one, following the same health precautions, particularly if the person died of a communicable disease.

In the United States, a doctor or coroner needs to sign a death certificate. It is not necessary that the doctor come to the deceased. For an expected death it is usually easiest to minister to the body before contacting the doctor about the death certificate. When you contact a crematorium or a burial society, they usually come soon. If you wish to let the body rest undisturbed, wait to contact these agencies. Make sure to remove jewelry before the body goes to the funeral home; it can be placed on the body again if desired.

In most places in the United States, family members or religious groups may serve as funeral directors.[2] A permit is required if you move the body yourself, and a burial or cremation document must be filed.[3]

An unembalmed body should be buried or cremated within several days to prevent bacteria from multiplying to unhealthy levels. Contrary to what many morticians suggest, embalming is not required unless the body is being shipped out of state, although many states require that the body be refrigerated within twenty-four to forty-eight hours after death. Be aware that embalming does not sterilize the body. The chemicals used in the embalming process are toxic to the living and are regulated by the government as hazardous materials. If you plan to digress from a conventional burial, investigate the laws in your area beforehand. You cannot depend on funeral parlors or hospital staff to help you figure out alternatives to normative procedures.

Burial on your own property is permitted in many places in the United States.[4] If home burial is chosen, keep in mind that future owners of the land may move the grave or may not permit it to be visited.

What is most important is to follow the wishes of the deceased.

FACING LOSS

Grief may push us into the hard question of "Why?" Why do I have to suffer like this? Why can't I get over it? Why did he have to die? Why is my heart so broken? Why?

In the tangled web of "Why?" we cannot find the reasons or words to make sense of our sadness. We can struggle with the feeling of being a pariah. We might feel that no one wants to be with a loser, with someone who has lost something she cherishes, be it a person or a life of quality. It is just too painful and reminds those around us that they are "losers" too.

Dying people can also grieve before they die. They can grieve in anticipation of their death for all they seem to be losing and what they have lost by being ill. Caregivers often grieve before those they care for have died. They are often saddened by the loss of freedom and options of those who are ill and the knowledge that death will rob them of one more relationship. Those left behind by the dying are often broken apart by the knowledge that they cannot bring back that which has been lost. The irrevocability of it all often leaves them helpless and sad. And there is also the particular grief of our culture that is conditioned only to possess . . . and not to let go.

We all face loss, but perhaps it is possible to accept it as a gift, albeit for most of us, a terrible gift. The brave practices that follow turn us toward our grief. They are short poems, affirmations, and prayers that keep us in the deep waters of grieving until grief is transmuted into feelings that give depth to our life.

In these practices, we are guided again and again to turn toward the arms of grief. This is being really brave. To deny grief is to rob ourselves of the heavy stones that will eventually be the ballast for our wisdom and compassion. When practicing these phrases, let the body settle; you can either sit or lie down. Remember why you are practicing; cultivate a tender heart. Then find a phrase or phrases that are appropriate to you and practice them with the breath or let your attention be gently with each phrase as you work with it.

Phrases for Loving-Kindness

May loving-kindness flow boundlessly.
May love and kindness fill and heal your body.
May the power of loving-kindness sustain you.
May you be peaceful in body and mind.

Phrases Nourishing Compassion

May you be free from pain and suffering.
May you take care of yourself.
May you be open to feel the pain in and around you.
May all beings be free from suffering.

Phrases for Engendering Sympathetic Joy

May all beings be happy.
May joy fill and sustain you.
May your well-being continue.
May you feel joy in your well-being.

Phrases That Foster Equanimity

All of us are the heirs of our actions.

Everyone must face her or his own situation.

Your happiness or unhappiness depend upon your
actions, not my wishes for you.

May you accept things as they are.

SEVENTEEN

Visualizations for Emotional Healing

by Tina L. Staley

THE PATH

The Preparation

I would like you to sit down and get comfortable in a chair. Take a moment and allow yourself to feel your weight being supported and held by that chair. Allow yourself to let go and to feel the chair pressing against your back, your buttocks sinking into your seat, and your feet planted firmly on the earth. Just let go and allow the chair to hold you.

Now, start letting go of what it took to get here. Let go of the conversations, the busyness of the mind, knowing that there is no right or wrong on how to do this. Know that thoughts will come in and out, and if they do, I would like you to simply focus your attention on your breath.

You can take your left hand now and put it on your abdomen and feel your belly expanding and contracting, expanding and contracting, expanding and contracting. I would like you to say to yourself, "soft belly, soft belly, soft belly." And as you are allowing the breath to move in and out, let go of the tension behind your eyes and forehead, allowing the jaw to relax, feeling your shoulders drop a little. Allow your arms and your hands to let go of their tension and feel a floating sensation. Allow the same letting go in your legs, releasing the energy moving through your muscles. Come back to your soft belly breathing, your soft belly.

The Path Exercise

Now I would like you to imagine yourself on a path; this can be a path that you have been on before, or it can be one that you have created in your own mind. And as you look around on the path, notice what time of year it is. What does the air feel like? What is the temperature? What are the colors you see? What is the light doing? What are the textures and sounds that you are seeing and hearing? As you move along your path, what is beneath your feet? What does the earth below you look like?

Now, as you walk you come to a bench. I would like for you to sit on the bench and relax, feeling the bench supporting you. Once again, while your body is continuing to be held, just look around you. Maybe you can hear the wind, possibly feel the sun, or see the birds. Just be present.

At this point, I would like you to invite a spirit guide to come and sit with you. The spirit guide may be someone you know, or it could possibly be an an animal spirit, a human spirit, or a divine spirit, but whoever it is, invite them to sit next to you. Think of a question you would like answered, then really begin to see this person: What does their face look like? What color eyes do they have? What color is their hair? Picture their mouth. Are they clothed? How are they clothed? And when you have this really clear, say what you need to say to this person. Is there anything else you would like to say to them? Truly feel the words coming from your heart, knowing that you can trust them.

And now, what would you like for them to tell you in return?

Know that you can call on your spirit guide anytime; know that they will always be there for you.

Now I would like you to say good-bye and to walk along your path, continuing to see the colors, the textures, the beauty, taking note of how you are feeling, knowing that you are loved and that you are all you need to be. Know that you are safe and that you are loved. You are loved.

And now come back to your soft belly, feeling your breath expand and contract, expand and contract. . . . When you are ready, slowly bring yourself back into the room. If you like, you can write down some notes of what you saw or felt, or hold them in yourself.

FORGIVENESS

The Preparation

I would like you to sit down and get comfortable in a chair. Take a moment and allow yourself to feel your weight being supported and held by that chair. Allow yourself to let go and to feel the chair pressing against your back, your buttocks sinking into your seat, and your feet planted firmly on the earth. Just let go and allow the chair to hold you.

Now, start letting go of what it took to get here. Let go of the conversations, the busyness of the mind, knowing that there is no right or wrong on how to do this. Know that thoughts will come in and out, and if they do, I would like you to simply focus your attention on your breath.

You can take your left hand now and put it on your abdomen and feel your belly expanding and contracting, expanding and contracting, expanding and contracting. I would like you to say to yourself, "soft belly, soft belly, soft belly." And as you are allowing the breath to move in and out, let go of the tension behind your eyes and forehead, allowing the jaw to relax, feeling your shoulders drop a little. Allow your arms and your hands to let go of their tension and feel a floating sensation. Allow the same letting go in your legs, releasing the energy moving through your muscles. Come back to your soft belly breathing, your soft belly.

The Forgiveness Exercise

Now I would like you to imagine yourself on a path; this can be a path that you have been on before, or it can be one that you have created in your own mind. And as you look around on the path, notice what time of year it is. What does the air feel like? What is the temperature? What are the colors you see? What is the lighting doing? What are the textures and sounds that you are seeing and hearing? As you move along your path, what is beneath your feet? What does the earth below you look like?

Now, as you walk, you come to a bench. I would like for you to sit on the bench and relax, feeling the bench supporting you. Once again, while your body is continuing to be held, just look around you. Maybe you can hear the wind, possibly feel the sun, or see the birds. Just be present.

At this point, I would like you to invite someone you would like to forgive to sit with you on your bench. Really see that person before you. What does their face look like? What color eyes do they have? Picture their mouth. What color is their hair?

Now ask what you would like to be forgiven for from that person. For instance, "I would like to be forgiven for _____."

After you have clearly expressed this, say what you would like to forgive them for. For instance, "I would like to forgive you for _____."

Now, forgive yourself, saying, "I would like to forgive myself for _____."

Thank the person and say, "I love you."

As you feel your heart expanding, you find yourself allowing the person to feel the forgiveness as well. And as you tell that person good-bye, know that you both are children of the Divine Wholeness, that you will move forward in the energy of love.

Now walk along the path, continuing to see the colors, the textures, the beauty, taking note of how you are feeling, knowing that you are all you need to be, knowing that you are safe, and that you are loved. You are loved. You are loved.

And now come back to your soft belly, feeling your breath expand and contract, expand and contract. . . . When you are ready, slowly bring yourself back into the room. If you like, you can write down some notes of what you saw or felt, or hold them in yourself.

LIGHT

The Preparation

I would like you to sit down and get comfortable in a chair. Take a moment and allow yourself to feel your weight being supported and held by that chair. Allow yourself to let go and to feel the chair pressing against your back, your buttocks sinking into your seat, and your feet planted firmly on the earth. Just let go and allow the chair to hold you.

Now, start letting go of what it took to get here. Let go of the conversations, the busyness of the mind, knowing that there is no right or wrong on how to do this. Know that thoughts will come in and out, and if they do, I would like you to simply focus your attention on your breath.

You can take your left hand now and put it on your abdomen and feel your belly expanding and contracting, expanding and contracting, expanding and contracting. I would like you to say to yourself, "soft belly, soft belly, soft belly." And as you are allowing the breath to move in and out, let go of the tension behind your eyes and forehead, allowing the jaw to relax, feeling your shoulders drop a little. Allow your arms and your hands to let go of their tension and feel a floating sensation. Allow the same letting go in your legs, releasing the energy moving through your muscles. Come back to your soft belly breathing, your soft belly.

The Exercise

I would like you to imagine a beautiful ball of healing light within yourself. What does the light look like? What color is it? What shape is it? Is it a soft glow or is it bright?

Feel this light within you, slowly expanding and taking over. The beautiful light is spreading itself through your cells, through your tissues, relaxing your nerves, and spreading through your bloodstream. As you feel this light within you, feel it expanding, penetrating your skin, and surrounding you. You are glowing in the beauty of this light within and without.

As you expand this light, imagine someone else you would also like to put this light around. Go ahead and allow them to feel this beautiful glow, this beautiful, beautiful light of love. Feel this beautiful light of love and grace filling your entire body and radiating outward. Be present with the love and light that surrounds you and surrounds this person, knowing that you have the ability when you meet this person or someone else, to bless them with this beautiful, loving, and healing light.

As you see this person, and as you see yourself in the grace of angelic love, know that you carry this light within you, and that at any moment you may rediscover what has always been there.

Now, come back to your soft belly, feeling your breath expand and contract, expand and contract. . . . When you are ready, slowly bring yourself back into the room. If you like, you can write down some notes of what you saw or felt, or hold them in yourself.

EIGHTEEN

Ministering to the Bereaved

by Mirabai Starr

Soon after September 11, 2001, my fourteen-year-old daughter, Jenny, was killed in a car accident. In that moment, the global grief I had been witnessing at a distance became intensely personal for me. I shared the pain of every mother everywhere—American, Afghani, Iraqi—as I struggled to bear the unbearable.

For a year or more, all I could do was tentatively face the fire of my feelings, offer quiet prayers for peace on the planet and in the hearts of all who were grieving. I sat amid the wreckage of my own heart, allowing the shattered fragments to reform according to the inscrutable timetable of the Divine, relinquishing any last illusions that I had control of anything in this life.

Eventually, like so many victims of tragedy, I turned my attention to service. This was the only path that made any sense. The ordinary concerns of daily life had dissolved in the inferno of my loss. Struck by the rarified awareness that had begun to grow in me, I became intensely interested in those whose own losses had acted as a catalyst for spiritual transformation in their lives.

What I noticed was that while many mourners had dedicated themselves to grief as a spiritual path, the culture at large did not affirm this choice or provide a framework for such a conversation. In spite of significant advances in death and dying education since the 1970s, American society on the whole still seems to suffer from fear and denial about the reality of death. In a culture where the casualties of our wars are invisible to the average citizen, where many of our elders are institutionalized, and where most of our ill pass away behind the closed doors of impersonal hospital rooms, we are becoming increasingly unfamiliar with one of the most natural and sacred functions of living: dying.

The death of a child is every parent's worst nightmare come true. When my daughter died, she was at the beginning of her blossoming, filled with indignation against injustice, hunger for justice, and the early flames of spiritual love. I had believed that Jenny would grow up to be someone who would make a conscious contribution to alleviating the suffering in this world. The loss of such potential, coupled with the primal agony of missing her, threatened to destroy me.

But there was another reality just beyond the edges of my anguish. A palpable sense of holiness began to pervade the emptiness carved by my shattering. As my family and community rallied to support me in those first hours and days of my loss, filling the air with their prayers and tears and singing, I noticed a radiance wash over my heart and the hearts of my circle of support. God was with us. And Jenny was with God. The exaltation accompanying this phenomenon confused me. The most terrible thing imaginable had happened, and while my suffering was acute, I was also being soothed and lifted by this ineffable holy joy.

As I began to sit with other mourners and listen to their stories, it became clear to me that I was not the only one who had experienced the sacred atmosphere that arises around the death of a loved one. I wondered how clergy people and spiritual leaders shepherded the souls in their care through the holy land of grief and loss.

I live in a small town in the mountains of northern New Mexico. Mine is a multicultural community, where Pueblo Indians, Chicanos, and "Anglos" (all others) have been living and dying together for generations. During the spring of 2004, I spoke with two Catholic priests, two Protestant pastors, one nondenominational minister, and the director of a grief and loss program about their experiences and views of the sacred passage of death in their respective congregations, in our community, and in society as a whole.

What I found among this diverse collection of spiritual guides was a unanimous commitment to "bearing witness" and "holding a container" for the bereaved to have his or her own experience of grief. In each case, the clergyperson consciously curtailed the impulse to fill the void of mystery with his own preconceived notions about the meaning of life and death. "Feelings," said Reverend John Snider, "are deeper than theology."

And yet, while they willingly released their grasp on the unknown and unknowable in the face of a death in their community, each of these clergy people stood on the solid ground of his or her own faith traditions. They all offered rituals, ceremonies, and prayers as a means of blessing the deceased and consoling the bereaved. "From an early age, a clear experience of the afterlife was always with me," says Father Bill McNichols, a Catholic priest and iconographer who worked with AIDS patients in New York

City throughout the 1980s. "I felt a friendship and communion with the saints. They were all dead, but I knew them as a living presence. This allowed me to unequivocally reassure those who were dying."

Clergy people are in the unique position to help those suffering from the death of a loved one to transform their loss into a profound spiritual experience. The religious leaders I spoke to shared with me that to do this, they have had to cultivate the humility and wisdom to step out of their own way, to resist the temptation to gloss over the mystery with platitudes or tell the mourners what to feel and how to grieve.

Dr. Janet Schreiber is the founding director of the Grief and Loss Certificate Program at Southwestern College in Santa Fe. When someone we love dies, Janet reminded me, grief can serve as a catalyst for a profound spiritual crisis. The ensuing shattering may cause us to question everything we believed about ourselves and our God. "Grief," says Janet, "is an experience of descent."

Clergy people can support the deep and important spiritual work that is taking place in this darkness. Rather than trying to console us with words, Janet suggests they can sit with us in the silence. Instead of trying to "make it better," they could simply stay with the reality of what is happening. Grievers are recreating themselves from the inside out. They need their clergy to bear witness to this sacred process, rather than to direct it according to their own unconscious fears and dogma. The spiritual leader may know from experience that the griever is going through a significant spiritual passage and that she will grow as a result, but he needs to keep this image in his own heart as he holds a safe and quiet place for the griever's own journey to unfold.

By placing too much emphasis on the sorrow and loss, a well-meaning spiritual guide might inadvertently disenfranchise a grieving person whose heart is overflowing with an inexplicable sweetness and connection to the divine, instilling in the bereaved a sense of shame that her experience is "bad" or "wrong." The Twenty-third Psalm, often recited at funerals, refers to "the valley of the shadow of death." Reverend Steve Wiard reminds his Methodist congregation that "you cannot have shadow without light!"

Reverend Ted Wiard (no relation to Steve Wiard) is the founding director of Golden Willow Retreat, a grief healing center outside of Taos. In the space of six years, Ted's brother Richard drowned in a fishing accident; his wife, Leslie, died of cancer; and his two daughters, Keri and Amy, were killed with their grandmother in a collision with a garbage truck. When well-meaning religious leaders tried to "fix" him with dogma, Ted rebelled. "There are no answers," Ted says of his shattering. "What I needed was to be held in a space of reverence and honoring."

Now, as a nondenominational minister and certified grief counselor, Ted provides this "holding" for others. The people who find their way to his isolated mountain retreat are invited to be present in the deeply sacred space that death has exploded in their lives, a place that words can't touch. "I have to have faith in people, that they are traveling their own sacred path, and that their higher power will help them. Who am I to take that away?" Ted asks. "I have no right not to hold that faith."

When Janet Schreiber and I sat together, we explored the notion of clergy people as "shepherds" of souls. "What is shepherding?" Janet mused. "If a sheep goes over the cliff, the shepherd climbs down into the chasm and hauls her back up. Otherwise, he just stays with them. Even if he has to hang out in places that are uncomfortable and unfamiliar, far from normal civilization."

It is not always easy to rise above ingrained attitudes about death and dying. Ministers, priests, and rabbis are just as subject to cultural conditioning as the rest of us. While we may project onto them some kind of omniscience with regard to the divine secrets, they too suffer from uncertainty and aversion. An honest, aware clergyperson will acknowledge his own relationship to death in the face of a loss in his congregation.

The day I met Father Bill at a local café to talk about his experiences with death, we encountered Father Tim Martinez just finishing his lunch, and we asked him to join us. The two men shared stories of the same deaths in their parish from their respective perspectives. As one recounted a particularly tragic incident, his eyes glistened with emotion, and I watched while compassion washed over the face of the other. "I'm grateful that we still feel pain and confusion, that we still feel close to it," Father Bill said. "Each time, we are really raw."

In the face of great distress, not all clergy people are skilled in allowing grieving people to fully feel their feelings. Our natural impulse is to soothe, to comfort, to relieve suffering. Reverend John Snider was a chaplain who earned the Silver Star during the Vietnam War. He witnessed mass casualties, sometimes daily. Throughout his forty-four-year career as a Presbyterian minister, he has performed hundreds of funerals.

But none of this experience prepared him for the recent death of his wife, Linda. "Suddenly, I am the one receiving solace," he told me. "And I'm finding that the simplest gestures console me. It's the simple recognition of my loss, to see that this person I loved was valued by my community."

All of the clergy people and grief counselors I spoke with bring the individual deaths they have experienced back into the context of the web of human connection. "It's important to remember that the death of an individual ripples out through the family and into the community," Ted pointed out. "Right now, we are experiencing global grief, on top of our individual losses. Those of us who have taken on ministerial work need to hold space for the whole human family that is experiencing the shattering of death and loss."

When my own child died, I instinctively reached for the mourning rituals of many different traditions. We brought Jenny's body home for twenty-four hours and held a vigil, singing Hindu *kirtan,* praying in Pali and Arabic, smudging her with cedar and sage, meditating in silence. Jenny's body was blessed by a Catholic priest before we took it to be cremated. Later, when we erected a Celtic cross as a *descanso* on the side of the road where Jenny was killed, Father Bill read a Taoist Kwan Yin prayer. In honor of my own heritage, we sat shivah and recited the Kaddish for seven days at sunset.

Fortunately, sensitive religious guides in each of these spiritual traditions made room for me to grieve in my own way, while supporting me with the depth of their faith. The wisdom and humility on the part of these clergy people enabled me to transform the death of my daughter from a sheer tragedy into something more than that, something that has grown my spirit.[1]

Acknowledgments

FIRST AND FOREMOST, we wish to thank the reader who has been courageous enough to read this work and to engage the difficult issues it treats. Thanks also to all those who participated in the Living Fully: Preparing for the End of Life and Beyond seminar in Aspen, Colorado, on July 9–11, 2004. We also wish to thank the original seminar speakers—Rabbi Zalman Schachter-Shalomi, Tessa Bielecki, Joan Halifax Roshi, Dr. Ira Byock, William Cathers, and Dr. Marilyn Schlitz—for their wonderful contributions. Included in this group should be Thomas Crum, who led breathing exercises during the breaks, and Eve Ilsen, who was originally slated to be a speaker but who could not come for dealing with the real-life application of these teachings with her mother, Sheba Penner, of blessed memory. We also wish to thank Jennifer and David Stockman, the Aspen Valley Community Foundation, and Chris Marsh, its executive director, who gave us generous support; Julia Jitkoff, our lovely and gracious host in Aspen, Colorado; Linda Johnson, who looked after us; and Deirdre Allen, who helped her. Thanks also to Iana Davis of Lafayette, Colorado, who transcribed the original tapes of the seminar; Tessa Bielecki, again, for supplying a number of the quotes; Dr. Michael Kearney for reading the work and providing feedback; Margi and Rick Hilleary, who hosted me while I was working in Glenwood Springs, Colorado; Jennifer Coffee, our acquisitions editor at Sounds True; Amy Hughes, our production editor; and Mirabai Starr who suggested Sounds True.

We would like to thank the Pathfinder team—Kristin MacDermott, Jerry Evans, Elizabeth Means, Dr. Amy Abernethy, Dr. Kim Lyerly, and Barbara Horne—and thanks to Jane Wheeler for her indispensable help. We are also deeply grateful to the Spiritual Paths board of directors: Reverend Gregg Anderson, John Bennett, Suzanne Farver, Jay Hughes, Judy Hyde, Margot Pritzker, John Sarpa, Michael Stranahan, Tina Staley, and Paula Zurcher. And we are especially appreciative of the wonderful work of Laura Dixon who so skillfully and gracefully managed the logistics of the Living-Fully seminar. Deep thanks also to Edgar Boyles for filming the whole event, Charles Abbot for his skillful photography, and Digital Arts Aspen for making video-editing equipment available for the edited video of the whole program. We are grateful to Lynn Goldsmith for providing wonderful photographic images of the speakers and participants.

We would like to thank our generous donors who helped fund Spiritual Paths and the program that is the basis for this book. First, we thank the Aspen Valley Medical Foundation and Pathfinders for their direct contributions for this book. And we deeply thank all the people listed alphabetically below who provided invaluable support: Theadora Bell, Deborah Bradford, Judy Burwell,

Mollie Campbell, Peter and Caroline Cavelti, Dennis and Dexter Cirillo, Pat Copper, Karen and Heinz Coordes, Susan Crown, Ester Devos, Macy and Leo Edelstein, Jim and Betsy Fifield, Charlie and Patti Firestone, Merrill Ford, Nancy Gensch, Lloyd Hermann, Christine Hibbard, Alberta Hogg, Susan Horsey, James Hughes, Holly Hunt, Julia Jitkoff, Tom Klutznick, Laurie MacCaskill, Kris Marsh, Maggie McVoy, Jackie Merrill, Jeannette Nichols, Laurie Pardee, Julie and Tom Paxton, Hensley and James Peterson, Carolyn Powers, Diane Rohlin, Carol Ruch, Jill Sabella, Jan Sarpa, Joe Scott, Victoria Simms, Jennifer Stockman, Mia Valley, Dennis and Linda Vaughn, Carolyn Walton, Lynda Weiser, Polly Whitcomb, George Wombell, and Julie Wycoff.

Finally, I would like to remember my father-in-law, Max Victor Phares (1948–2008), who died during the final preparation of this book, and through whom—with family and friends surrounding him—I was privileged to witness why this book is so important.

NETANEL MILES-YEPEZ, EDITOR
Boulder, Colorado, 2009

Notes

Introduction

1. Many years later I joked with Geshe-la about his constant refrain, "If I don't die." I said, "You have been saying this for years, but you're still alive!" To which he replied with a grin, "It is not easy to die!" In his prayers, visualizations, meditations, chants, and daily life, Geshe-la is always transforming himself into a wise, compassionate, and eternal Buddha. He is living fully in every moment, always shedding the illusions of his false self, always seeing the truth of existence around him, always ready to lend a helping hand, and always engaged with compassion and humor with everyone he meets. To me he is the living personification of living fully and dying well.

2. The Way of Contemplation and Meditation was followed by The Way of the Mystic and The Way of Devotion and Faith.

3. Tina brings unbounded energy, joy, compassion, dedication, and intelligence to her work. She is loved by our whole community of patients, families, doctors, and staff. Because of her deep empathy and skillful presence, all of us who know her would like her to be with us as we near the end of our life. Fortunately, her work and presence are felt far beyond the beautiful town and valley of Aspen, Colorado.   —*E.B.*

Part I, One

1. Levine, Stephen, and Ondrea Levine. *Who Dies? An Investigation of Conscious Living and Conscious Dying.* New York: Anchor, 1989.

2. Robert A. F. Thurman is a professor of Indo-Tibetan Buddhist Studies in the Department of Religion at Columbia University and president of the Tibet House U.S. and the American Institute of Buddhist Studies. He is the author of *The Tibetan Book of the Dead* and *Inner Revolution: Life, Liberty, and the Pursuit of Real Happiness* and *Infinite Life: Seven Virtues for Living Well.* However, this quote may have originally come from Ram Dass.

3. This experiment was done at the Living Fully: Preparing for the End of Life and Beyond conference in Aspen, Colorado, with these very results.

4. Genesis 25:8. In the *JPS English-Hebrew Tanak* (p. 47), it says, "And Abraham breathed his last, dying at a good ripe age, old and contented; and he was gathered to his kin."

5. Psalms 91:16. In the *JPS English-Hebrew Tanak* (p. 1528), it says, "I will let him live to a ripe old age, and show him my salvation."

6. This is referring to the "reptilian complex" or "R-complex," which is part of the triune brain model proposed by Dr. Paul D. MacLean. His theory seeks to explain brain function through the evolution of existing structures of the human brain. Thus, his model of the triune brain consists of (1) the R-complex (also known as the brainstem), (2) the limbic system, and (3) the neocortex.

7. Dr. Elisabeth Kübler-Ross (1926–2004) was a Swiss-born psychiatrist and the author of the seminal work *On Death and Dying,* in which she first discussed what is now known as "the Kübler-Ross model" and the five stages through which people deal with grief and tragedy. These stages, also called The Five Stages of Grief, are (1) denial, (2) anger, (3) bargaining, (4) depression, and (5) acceptance.

8. This is a part of the core philosophy of "Spiritual Eldering" taught by The Sage-ing Guild, an organization of teachers basing themselves on Schachter-Shalomi's teachings. See Schachter-Shalomi, Zalman, and Ronald S. Miller. *From Ageing to Sage-ing: A Profound New Vision of Growing Older.* New York: Warner Books, 1995.

Part I, Two

1. This is a quote from Father William McNamara, a Discalced Carmelite monk and cofounder, along with Tessa Bielecki, of the Spiritual Life Institute, with monasteries in Crestone, Colorado, and County Sligo, Ireland. He is the author of *Christian Mysticism: The Art of the Inner Way* (Continuum, 1995) and *Mystical Passion: The Art of Christian Loving* (Element, 1991).

2. St. Teresa of Avila, *Soliloquies 6.2.*

3. Mother Tessa prefers the term "monk" to "nun," and occasionally used to call herself a "nunk." The word "monk" comes from the Greek *monachos,* which simply means "one who lives alone," though monks live in an intentional community under the guidance of a "rule." Today, Tessa Bielecki lives as a hermitess in a small hermitage in Crestone, Colorado.

4. Sufism is a mystical path of spiritual experience that originally evolved out of Islam. Today, there are both Muslim Sufis and Universalist Sufis (from the lineage of Hazrat Inayat Khan [1882–1927]).

5. The Sufi sheikh Abu Hamid al-Ghazzali (1058–1111) said that in his *Alchemy of Happiness.*

6. The term "holarchy" is most often used by the philosopher Ken Wilber in order to get away from "hierarchy" and to be more accurate in describing "nested realities" that tend to "transcend and include" as they evolve.

7. Jalaluddin Rumi (1207–1273) was a Muslim-Sufi mystic and poet. He was the (posthumous) founder of the Mevlevi Sufi tradition and the author of the great Farsi spiritual classic known as the *Mathnawi.* Today, his poetry in various English translations is among the most popular in the English-speaking world.

8. Shanti-Nilaya retreat was founded by Elisabeth Kübler-Ross in the 1970s in Escondido, California. It was nearly destroyed by a fire in 1983.

9. *Pranayama* is a Sanskrit word for breathing techniques that move the subtle energy (*prana*) carried on the breath.

10. *Chi* or *ki* are the Chinese and Japanese, respectively, for what is known as *prana* in Sanskrit. See previous note.

11. Kundalini in Hindu and Buddhist Tantric philosophy refers to a coiled energy residing at the base of the spine in the subtle body that (through various practices) is released and rises, awakening the chakras (centers of awareness) as it ascends.

12. Matthew 26:37–39.

13. St. John Chrysostom (ca. 400 C.E.), pastor of Constantinople, in his *Easter Sermon*.

Part I, Three

1. In 1968, Dr. Lawrence Weed published a paper outlining his Problem-Oriented Medical Record (POMR) that was subsequently adopted in most medical facilities and is today considered a major contribution to medical charting.

2. The APGAR Score was created in 1952 by Dr. Virginia Apgar to easily assess the health of newborn children. In 1963, a pediatrician named Dr. Joseph Butterfield created a mnemonic from the name Apgar which correlated to Virginia Apgar's five criteria for assessing health in the neonate: Appearance (skin color), Pulse (heart rate), Grimace (reflex irritability), Activity (muscle tone), and Respiration.

3. "Hospitalism" was a pediatric diagnosis used in the 1930s to describe infants who "failed to thrive" while in hospital. The

symptoms often included retarded physical development and disruption of perceptual-motor skills and language. It is now understood that this "wasting" disease was mostly caused by a lack of social contact between the infant and its caregivers.

4. René Árpád Spitz (1887–1974) was an American psychoanalyst of Hungarian origin who worked at the University of Denver. His primary interest was in the relationship between mother and child.

5. The Pew-Fetzer Task Force on Psychosocial Health Education was formed to serve in an advisory capacity to the Pew Health Professions Commission and the Fetzer Institute in the development of an agenda for encouraging the development or expansion of educational programs that reflect an integrated biomedical-psychosocial perspective.

Part I, Four

1. Dr. Balfour Mount (b. 1939) is a Canadian physician, surgeon, and academic, considered to be one of the fathers of palliative care in North America.

2. Dr. John F. Scott is trained in medicine, theology, and clinical epidemiology and has been active in the palliative care field since 1975. From 1978 to 1988, he was the director of Palliative Care Services in hospitals in Montreal, Toronto, and Hamilton, Ontario.

3. The Spitzer Quality of Life Index was designed as an objective index for use by physicians to enhance quality of life in patients with terminal cancer.

4. Melanie P. Merriman, Ph.D., M.B.A., is the founder of Touchstone Consulting in North Bay Village, Florida, a firm that specializes in health-care quality and outcomes management and program evaluation.

5. The Missoula-Vitas Quality of Life Index can be found on Dr. Ira Byock's Web site: www.dyingwell.org.

6. Gerald Jampolsky, M.D., is a psychiatrist, formerly on the faculty of the University of California Medical Center in San Francisco. He is the founder of the Center for Attitudinal Healing in Sausalito, California, and a fellow of the American Psychiatric Association.

7. Pathfinders at Duke University Medical Center is a program designed to address the mind, body, and spiritual needs of each individual cancer patient.

8. Dr. Keith Block is the medical director at the Block Center for Integrative Cancer Care in Evanston, Illinois.

Part I, Five

1. *DSM-IV* (*Diagnostic and Statistical Manual of Mental Disorders*, 4th Edition) is a manual published by the American Psychiatric Association (APA) that includes all currently recognized mental health disorders.

2. Ram Dass (formerly known as Dr. Richard Alpert) (b. 1931) is a spiritual teacher and disciple of the Hindu guru Neem Karoli Baba. He was first famous as the experimental collaborator of Dr. Timothy Leary, researching the effects of LSD on consciousness. Later, he abandoned that career and became a well-known

spiritual teacher and bestselling author. Two of his books are *Be Here Now* and *Still Here: Embracing Aging, Changing, and Dying.*

3. Stephen Levine is a poet and teacher of guided meditation healing techniques. He and his wife and spiritual partner, Ondrea, have counseled the dying and their loved ones for more than thirty years. Stephen Levine's bestselling books *Healing into Life and Death, A Gradual Awakening,* and *A Year to Live* are considered classics in the field of conscious living and dying. He is also the coauthor, with Ondrea, of the acclaimed *To Love and Be Loved* and *Who Dies?*

4. Sir Walter Scott (1771–1832), Scottish novelist and poet. This very popular quote says, "Death—the last sleep? No, it is the final awakening."

5. Tetsugen Bernie Glassman is a Roshi of the Soto Zen Buddhist lineage, a student of Maezumi Roshi, and is widely known for his influential books *Bearing Witness* and *Instructions to the Cook.* He is the founder (with Roshi Jishu Holmes) of the Zen Peacemaker Order (1996), which bases itself on three principles: plunging into the unknown, bearing witness to the pain and joy of the world, and commiting to heal oneself and the world.

6. According to Robert Thurman, traditional Buddhist scholars believe Vimalakirti to be "an emanated incarnation (*nirmanakaya*) of the Buddha, *a living allegory,*" whose teaching is collected in the brilliant *Vimalakirtinirdeshasutra* (*The Holy Teaching of Vimalakirti,* p. 9).

7. Attention Deficit Disorder.

8. Chagdud Tulku Rinpoche (1930–2002) was a renowned teacher of the Nyingma school of Tibetan Vajrayana Buddhism and author of *Lord of the Dance.*

Part I, Six

1. Emmanuel Swedenborg (1688–1772) was a Swedish scientist, philosopher, Christian mystic, and theologian. His most famous work is *Heaven and Hell*.

2. Rebbe is a term used in Hasidic Judaism for a spiritual master, the leader of a group of Hasidim, spiritual seekers.

3. Rabbi Joseph Isaac Schneersohn (1880–1950) was the sixth dynastic leader of the HaBaD-Lubavitch lineage of Hasidism. He was Rabbi Zalman Schachter-Shalomi's teacher from 1941 to 1950.

4. In Jewish mystical thought, it is thought that there are an infinite number of Worlds. However, these may be broken down into four basic Worlds: the World of Action, the World of Feeling, the World of Knowing, and the World of Being.

5. The Tibetan word *bardo* literally means "intermediate," "transitional," or "in-between state."

6. The work commonly known in English as *The Tibetan Book of the Dead* is called in Tibetan, *Bardo Thodol* (liberation through hearing in the intermediate state). This famous funerary text describes the experiences of the consciousness after death during the interval known as bardo between death and rebirth.

7. Deuteronomy 11:21. In the *JPS English-Hebrew Tanak* (p. 400), it says, "to the end that you and your children may endure, in the land that the LORD swore to your fathers to assign to them, as long as there is a heaven over the earth."

8. Eugene Jeffrey (E. J.) Gold (b. 1941) is an artist, author, jazz musician, and spiritual teacher.

9. Gold, E. J. *The American Book of the Dead*. Nevada City, CA: Gateways, 1999.

10. Psalms 139:1–3. In the *JPS English-Hebrew Tanak* (p. 1585), it says, "O Lord, You have examined me and know me. When I sit down or stand up You know it; You discern my thoughts from afar. You observe my walking and my reclining, and are familiar with all my ways."

11. Dante Alighieri (1265–1321), an Italian poet from Florence, whose central work, *The Divine Comedy,* is considered the greatest literary work composed in the Italian language and a masterpiece of world literature.

12. Paul Gustave Doré (1832–1883) was a French artist, engraver, and illustrator who illustrated Dante's *The Divine Comedy*.

13. Hieronymus Bosch (pseudonym of Jheronimus van Aken) (c. 1450–1516) was a prolific Dutch painter who often used images of demons, half-human animals, and machines to evoke fear and confusion to portray the evil of human beings.

14. Meshullam Zushya of Anipol (d. 1800) was a third-generation Hasidic master.

15. Much of this material is contained in Simcha Raphael's (a student of Reb Zalman's) remarkable book *Jewish Views of the Afterlife* (Jason Aronson, 1994).

16. Daniel 7:10. In the *JPS English-Hebrew Tanak* (p. 1822), it says, "A river of fire streamed forth before Him."

17. *Star Trek* is an American science fiction television and movie series created by Gene Roddenberry in 1966.

18. The recitation of the Rosary is traditionally dedicated to one of three sets of "Mysteries": the Joyful Mysteries, the Sorrowful Mysteries, and the Glorious Mysteries. Each of these three sets of Mysteries has within it five different sacred themes related to the life of Jesus.

19. *The Chronicles of Narnia* is a series of seven fantasy novels for children written by C. S. Lewis.

20. Hildegard von Bingen (1098–1179) was a German Benedictine *magistra*, artist, author, counselor, dramatist, linguist, naturalist, philosopher, physician, poet, political consultant, prophet, visionary, and a composer of music.

21. Teresa of Avila (1515–1582) was a prominent Spanish mystic, writer, and monastic reformer. Tessa Bielecki belongs to the Carmelite Order founded by Teresa of Avila.

22. Francis of Assisi (1181–1226) was a Roman Catholic friar and the founder of the Order of Friars Minor, more commonly known as the Franciscans.

23. The Rosary (Latin, *rosarium,* "rose garden") is a traditional devotion in the Roman Catholic Church. The term denotes both a set of prayer beads and a set of prayers to be said.

24. Jacques Maritain. "Action and Contemplation." In *Scholasticism and Politics.* Garden City, New York: Doubleday Image, 1960: p. 182.

25. Matthew 13:24–30. In the New English Bible with the Apocrypha (p. 19), it says, "A man sowed his field with good seed; but while everyone was asleep his enemy came, sowed darnel among the wheat, and made off. When the corn sprouted and began to fill out, the darnel could be seen among it. The farmer's men went to their master and said, 'Sir, was it not good seed that you sowed in your field? Then where has the darnel come from?' 'This is the enemy's doing,' he replied. 'Well then,' they said, 'shall we go and gather the darnel?' 'No,' he answered, 'in gathering it you might pull up the wheat at the same time.'"

26. The term "mythopoeia" was developed by J. R. R. Tolkien and refers to the human cocreational process of myth-making with the divine.

27. Carl Gustav Jung (1875–1961) was a Swiss psychiatrist, influential thinker, and founder of analytical psychology.

Part I, Seven

1. The Institute of Noetic Sciences (IONS) was founded in 1973 by former astronaut Edgar Mitchell to encourage and conduct research and education programs on mind-body relationships for the purpose of expanding "human possibility by investigating aspects of reality—mind, consciousness, and spirit."

2. Dean Radin is a researcher and author in the field of parapsychology. He is senior scientist at the Institute of Noetic Sciences in Petaluma, California; on the adjunct faculty at Sonoma State University; on the distinguished consulting faculty at Saybrook Graduate School and Research Center; and former president of the Parapsychological Association.

3. Gary E. Schwartz, Ph.D., is a professor of psychology at the University of Arizona. He is also the director of The VERITAS Research Program of the Human Energy Systems Laboratory. Dr. Schwartz's major research focus has been in the field of parapsychology.

4. Florence Nightingale (1820–1910), who came to be known as The Lady of the Lamp, was a pioneer of modern nursing, a writer, and a noted statistician.

5. Electroencephalography is the neurophysiologic measurement of the electrical activity of the brain by recording from electrodes placed on the scalp or, in special cases, subdurally or in the cerebral cortex. The resulting traces are known as an electroencephalogram (EEG).

Part I, Eight

1. Ian Pretyman Stevenson, M.D., (1918–2007) was a Canadian-American psychiatrist whose research interests included children who claim to remember previous lives, near-death experiences, apparitions (death-bed visions), the mind-brain problem, and survival of the human personality after death.

2. The word "Torah" means "teaching" in Hebrew and corresponds specifically to the Five Books of Moses, but is also inclusive of all teaching in Judaism.

3. Gershom, Yonassan. *Beyond the Ashes: Cases of Reincarnation from the Holocaust.* Virginia Beach: A.R.E. Press, 1992.

4. The term "Kaddish" is often used to refer specifically to "The Mourners' Kaddish," said as part of the mourning rituals in Judaism in all prayer services, as well as at funerals and memorials.

Part I, Nine

1. I called my daughter, Alexandra, to let her know what was happening and asked her to let our family know what was happening. Even though she offered to come up to Santa Barbara from Claremont, where she was attending graduate school, I didn't want her to have to go through that trouble and to miss her classes. Later I wished she had been there.

2. I began looking for a good doctor, since my attending resident interns didn't give me much confidence in their knowledge and experience. The attending emergency room physician had been pulled away by other emergencies, so I lay there alone, feeling the morphine kicking in and wondering when they would begin injecting me with the blood thinner for my clots. Luckily, my cell phone was working and I was able to reach my friend Stacy Buck, who, with my buddy Nancy Bell Coe, was able to locate a wonderful physician and human being named Dr. John Lynn, who dropped everything, came to my assistance, and hooked me up with Dr. Rob Wright, the head of pulmonology.

3. The chakra (Sanskrit, "wheel"), according to Hindu and Buddhist thought, is a subtle-body nexus that may be "awakened," releasing a flow of energy to the next chakra. There are said to be seven chakras in the human body.

4. A bodhisattva is an enlightened being who, out of compassion for all beings, chooses to be reborn into the cycle birth and death (with all of its pain and suffering) for the purpose of helping all beings to attain Enlightenment.

5. An apophatic theology or practice sees divinity as ineffable, inexpressible, and therefore attempts to describe it in terms of what

it is not. Apophatic statements refer to transcendence in this context, as opposed to cataphatic statements referring to divine immanence. This is why it is called a *via negativa* approach.

6. A mantra is a sacred formula or word repeated over and over as a means of invoking a particular sacred intention or to aid concentration.

7. Tantra (Sanskrit, "weave") has to do with those higher-level teachings and practices that help us to integrate the specifically spiritual with the material aspects of our lives. Contrary to its popular modern usage, tantra has nothing to do with sex in an exclusive way, except that sex is among the material aspects of life with which tantra deals.

8. In the Christian Carmelite community at Nada Hermitage in Crestone, Colorado, part of the Spiritual Life Institute that Tessa Bielecki founded, and to which she used to belong. She now lives nearby as a hermit.

9. Viktor Emil Frankl, M.D., Ph.D., (1905–1997) was an Austrian neurologist and psychiatrist as well as a Holocaust survivor. Frankl was the founder of Logotherapy and Existential Analysis. His book *Man's Search for Meaning* chronicles his experiences as a concentration camp inmate and describes his psychotherapeutic method of finding meaning in all forms of existence, even the most difficult.

10. Thich Nhat Hanh (b. 1926) is an expatriate Vietnamese Zen Buddhist monk, teacher, author, and peace activist.

11. Terry Tempest Williams (b. 1955) is an American author, naturalist, and environmental activist.

12. Rainer Maria Rilke (1875–1926) is considered one of the twentieth century's greatest poets.

13. Schlitz, Marilyn, Tina Amorok, and Marc Micozzi. *Consciousness and Healing: Integral Approaches to Mind-Body Medicine.* Churchill-Livingstone, 2004.

14. Kenneth Earl (Ken) Wilber (b. 1949) is an American author and perhaps the most widely influential philosopher alive today.

15. Schlitz, Marilyn, Cassandra Vieten, and Tina Amorok. *Living Deeply: The Art and Science of Transformation in Everyday Life.* Berkeley, CA: New Harbinger, 2008.

16. Blaise Pascal (1623–1662) was a French mathematician, physicist, and religious philosopher.

17. Tenzin Wangyal Rinpoche is a lama of the Bon Tibetan religious tradition and the author of *The Tibetan Yogas of Dream and Sleep.* Ithaca, New York: Snow Lion Publications, 1998.

18. Stillwater, Michael, and Gary Malkin. *Graceful Passages: A Companion for Living and Dying* (2 CDs with Book). Perf. Ram Dass, Lew Epstein, Arun Gandhi, Sunanda Gandhi, Thich Nhat Hanh, Alan Jones, Jyoti, Maximillian Mizzi, Elisabeth Kübler-Ross, Zalman Schachter-Shalomi, Tu Wei Ming, Michael Stillwater. Prod. Michael Stillwater and Gary Malkin. Greenbrae, California: Wisdom of the World, 2000.

19. Rabbi Menachem Mendel Schneersohn (1902–1994) was the seventh dynastic leader of the HaBaD-Lubavitch lineage of Hasidism.

20. Reb Zalman added at the end of the dialogue: "As far as a bene-diction or a blessing is concerned, I want to say, everybody who gets older has to learn how to give blessings. And the thing to know is that it is not *you* doing it. It is as if you are reaching up to a divine deposit above you, and just bringing it down. So if I think of God as Mother, giving a blessing is like letting the milk come down, but you have to do the sucking yourself!"

Part II, Fifteen

1. Joan Halifax wishes to thank the late Chagdud Tulku Rinpoche, His Holiness the Dalai Lama, and the late Diane Shainberg for help with this practice.

Part II, Sixteen

1. Joan Halifax learned about this practice from Patricia Shelton and Richard Boerstler, who developed a practice called "co-meditation" based on teachings from the late Tibetan teacher Chogyam Trungpa Rinpoche. She has simplified the practice according to her own experience of sharing it with others.

2. Not true at this time in Indiana.

3. See county health department.

4. It's recommended that you put a $25,000 amount in trust. Contact local health department.

Part II, Eighteen

1. Previously published as "Shepherds in the Night: Ministering to the Bereaved." *Sojourners Magazine.* November 2004.

A Selected Reading List

Becker, Ernst. *The Denial of Death*. Free Press, 1997.

Bielecki, Tessa. *Holy Daring: An Outrageous Gift to Modern Spirituality from Saint Teresa, the Grand Wild Woman of Avila*. Element Books, 1994.

Bielecki, Tessa (Ed.). *Teresa of Avila: Ecstasy and Common Sense*. Shambhala, 1996.

Bielecki, Tessa (Ed.). *Teresa of Avila: Mystical Writings*. Crossroads Classics, 1994.

Boros, Ladislaus. *Pain and Providence*. Trans. Edward Quinn. Helicon, 1966.

Bourgeault, Cynthia. *Centering Prayer and Inner Awakening*. Cowley Publications, 2004.

Byock, Ira. *Dying Well: Peace and Possibilities at the End of Life*. Riverhead Trade, 1998.

Byock, Ira. *The Four Things That Matter Most: A Book about Living*. Free Press, 2004.

Callanan, Maggie. *Final Gifts: Understanding the Special Awareness, Needs, and Communications of the Dying.* Bantam, 1992.

Dalai Lama. *Advice on Dying and Living a Better Life.* Atria Books, 2002.

Dalai Lama. *Sleeping, Dreaming and Dying.* Wisdom Publications, 1997.

Day, Dorothy. *The Long Loneliness.* Harper Row, 1952.

Doore, Gary. *What Survives? Contemporary Explorations of Life after Death.* Tarcher, 1990.

Feinstein, David, and Peg Mayo. *Rituals for Living and Dying.* Harper Collins, 1990.

Foos-Graber, Anya. *Deathing.* Nicolas-Hays, 1989.

Gaines, Ernest J. *A Lesson Before Dying.* Vintage, 1997.

Gershom, Yonassan. *Beyond the Ashes: Cases of Reincarnation from the Holocaust.* A.R.E. Press, 1992.

Gold, E. J. *The American Book of the Dead.* Gateway Books, 1999.

Grof, Stanislov, and Joan Halifax. *The Human Encounter with Death.* Penguin, 1978.

Gunther, John. *Death Be Not Proud.* Harper Perennial, 1998.

Halifax, Joan. *Being with Dying: Cultivating Compassion and Fearlessness in the Presence of Death.* Shambhala, 2008.

Halifax, Joan. *The Fruitful Darkness: Reconnecting with the Body of the Earth.* Harper Collins, 1994.

Halifax, Joan. *Shaman: The Wounded Healer.* Crossroad Publishing Company, 1983.

de Hennezel, Marie. *Intimate Death.* Vintage, 1998.

Kapleau, Philip. *The Wheel of Death.* Harper and Row, 1971.

Karen, Robert. *The Forgiving Self: The Road from Resentment to Connection.* Random House, 2001.

Kearney, M. *Mortally Wounded: Stories of Soul Pain, Death, and Healing.* Scribner, 1996.

Kearney, M. "Palliative Medicine—Just Another Specialty?" *Palliative Medicine.* Vol. 6, 1992: pp. 39–46.

Kearney, M. *A Place of Healing: Working with Suffering in Living and Dying.* Oxford University Press, 2000.

Kearney, M. "Spiritual Pain." *The Way.* Vol. 30, No. 1, 1990: pp. 47–54.

Kearney, M., and B. Mount. "Healing and Palliative Care: Charting Our Way Forward." *Palliative Medicine.* Vol. 17, 2003: pp. 657–658.

Kearney, M., and B. Mount. "Spiritual Care of the Dying Patient." *Handbook of Psychiatry in Palliative Medicine.* Eds. H. M. Chochinov and W. Breitbart. Oxford University Press, 2000: pp. 357–373.

Kramer, Kenneth. *The Sacred Art of Dying: How World Religions Understand Death.* Paulist Press, 1988.

Kübler-Ross, Elisabeth. *On Death and Dying.* Scribner, 1997.

Kübler-Ross, Elisabeth, and David Kessler. *On Grief and Grieving.* Scribner, 2005.

Lati Rimpoche and Jeffrey Hopkins. *Death, Intermediate State, and Rebirth.* Snow Lion, 1980.

Levine, Stephen, and Ondrea Levine. *Who Dies? An Investigation of Conscious Living and Conscious Dying.* Anchor, 1989.

Lewis, C. S. *The Great Divorce.* Touchstone, Simon and Schuster, 1996.

Lewis, C. S. *A Grief Observed.* Harper and Row, 1961.

Lewis, C. S. *The Last Battle.* Macmillan, 1956.

Maull, Fleet. *Dharma in Hell: The Prison Writings of Fleet Maull.* Prison Dharma Network, 2005.

Mullin, Glenn H. *Death and Dying: The Tibetan Tradition.* Penguin, 1986.

Neeld, Elizabeth Harper. *Seven Choices: Finding Daylight after Loss Shatters Your World.* Warner Books, 2003.

Newman, John Henry. *The Dream of Gerontius.* Family Publications, 2001.

Nouwen, Henri J. M. *Our Greatest Gift: A Meditation on Dying and Caring.* Harper San Francisco, 1994.

Nuland, Sherwin. *How We Die: Reflection on Life's Final Chapter.* Vintage, 1995.

Raphael, Simcha Paull. *Jewish Views of the Afterlife.* Foreword by Zalman M. Schachter-Shalomi. Jason Aronson, 1994.

Ram Dass. *Paths to God: Living the Bhagavad Gita.* Harmony, 2004.

Ram Dass. *Still Here: Embracing Aging, Changing, and Dying.* Riverhead Books, 2001.

Schachter-Shalomi, Zalman. *Spiritual Intimacy: A Study of Counseling in Hasidism.* Jason Aronson, 1991.

Schachter-Shalomi, Zalman. *Wrapped in a Holy Flame: Teachings and Tales of the Hasidic Masters.* Ed. N. Miles-Yepez. Jossey-Bass, 2003.

Schachter-Shalomi, Zalman, and Netanel Miles-Yepez. *A Heart Afire: Stories and Teachings of the Early Hasidic Masters.* Jewish Publication Society, 2009.

Schachter-Shalomi, Zalman, and Ronald S. Miller. *From Age-ing to Sage-ing: A Profound New Vision of Growing Older.* Warner Books, 1995.

Schachter-Shalomi, Zalman, with Joel Segel. *Jewish with Feeling: A Guide to a Meaningful Jewish Practice.* Riverhead Books, 2005.

Schlitz, Marilyn, Tina Amorok, and Marc Micozzi. *Consciousness and Healing: Integral Approaches to Mind-Body Medicine.* C.V. Mosby, 2004.

Singh, Kathleen Dowling. *The Grace in Dying: A Message of Hope, Comfort, and Spiritual Transformation*. Harper San Francisco, 1998.

Smedes, Lewis. *Forgive and Forget: Healing the Hurts We Don't Deserve*. Harper Collins, 1996.

Sogyal Rinpoche. *The Tibetan Book of Living and Dying*. Harper Collins, 1993.

Thondup, Tulku. *Peaceful Death, Joyous Rebirth: A Tibetan Buddhist Guidebook*. Shambhala, 2005.

Thurman, Robert (Trans.). *The Tibetan Book of the Dead*. Bantam Books, 1993.

Webb, Marilyn. *A Good Death: The New American Search to Reshape the End of Life*. Bantam, 1999.

Wooten-Green, Ron. *When the Dying Speak: How to Listen to and Learn from Those Facing Death*. Loyola Press, 2001.

Index

N

Nada Hermitage, 263n8

Nahar deNur (River of Light), 81–82

Narnia, 72, 73, 84, 87, 88

National Center for Complementary and Alternative Medicine, 93

National Hospice and Palliative Care Organization, 32–33

National Institutes of Health, 93

near-death experiences, 82, 100–102, 112–113, 134

New Testament, 85–86

Nichols, Jeannette, 247

Nightingale, Florence, 99, 261n4

Noble Truths, 122–123

Nomad Clinic, 122

nonlocal consciousness, 93–102

nonlocal healing. *see* distant healing

not knowing, 67

Nouwen, Henri J. M., 3

nurses, 37. *see also* caregivers; health-care professionals

nursing homes
fear of dying in, 28–41
geriatric failure to thrive syndrome, 34

Nyingma school, 256n8

O

obedience, 18

objectivity, 25–26

openness, 67, 69

orphanages, 33–34

others, 69. *see also* relationships

outer world, 37–38

P

pain, 67. *see also* suffering
acceptance of, 182–183
avoidance of, 79
in Buddhism, 67, 122
caregivers and, 121, 124–125
dealing with, 119
eliminating, 119
managing, 119–120
objectivifying, 68
observation of, 68
practices for working with, 68
relief of, 35
transforming, 179–186

palliative care, 32, 35, 55, 124–125, 128, 129, 293. *see also* health-care professionals

Paradise, 81–82, 85–86, 142. *see also* the afterlife; Garden of Eden; Heaven

Pardee, Laurie, 247

Pascal, Blaise, 136, 264n16

Pascal's wager, 136

Paschal Mystery, 17–18

Passover Mystery, 17–18

About the Authors

Dr. Edward W. Bastian earned a Ph.D. in Buddhist studies and Western philosophy from the University of Wisconsin. He conducted research using Tibetan and Sanskrit languages for a number of years in India as a Fulbright Fellow and recipient of grants and fellowships from the Smithsonian and the American Institute of Indian Studies. In India, he lived in Tibetan monasteries and studied Indian philosophy and religion at Banares Hindu University. He has taught courses and moderated discussions on religion for the Smithsonian on Buddhism and world religions. He also has taught and lectured at a variety of educational venues and presented scholarly papers and films at academic conferences in the United States, England, Japan, and India.

Bastian was the executive producer for a series of six award-winning television programs on religion in India, Bhutan, and Japan for the BBC, and produced a series of three films on Tibetan Buddhism with funding from the National Endowment for the

Humanities, the U.S. Office of Education, and the Smithsonian Institution. The production of these films drew heavily on the expertise of indigenous scholars, and the films have been generally recognized for their sensitivity, depth, and authenticity.

Bastian has directed several nonprofit organizations and has been a business executive, most recently as president of Aspen.com, an Internet company in Colorado. He also consults with spiritual institutions and media organizations and sits on various nonprofit and public interest boards. Presently, he is president of Spiritual Paths Foundation, which is producing seminars, books, television programs, and a Web site on spirituality, based on a methodology he has developed in collaboration with authentic exemplars from the world's major spiritual traditions.

Tina L. Staley, M.S.W., L.C.S.W., holds a bachelor of arts degree in psychology and a master's degree in clinical social work from Loyola University. She was the director of the Cancer Guide Program at Aspen Valley Hospital, the national spokesperson for eating disorders on the board of Anorexia Nervosa and Associated Disorders, a founder of the Aspen Center for Integral Health, on the faculty for Mind-Body Medicine, and on the board of directors of the Roaring Fork Hospice and the Spiritual Paths Foundation.

Currently, Tina is the director of Pathfinders (an integrative, whole-person approach to cancer care addressing the mind, body, and spiritual needs of each individual cancer patient, working side by side with a medical team) at Duke University Medical Center in Durham, North Carolina. Working as a member of a medical-social science research team at Duke University Medical Center, Tina is developing new quality-of-life care interventions and assessing their benefits for patients and their families, specifically patients with advanced breast cancer. These assessments consider the cancer patients' psychosocial needs and their response to supportive interventions. She is also collaborating with nursing administration on approaches to improving institutional support for nursing stress management and self-care, as well as educating student nurses on preparing patients and families for end of life.

Contributors

Tessa Bielecki was (until 2005) cofounder and Mother Abbess of the Spiritual Life Institute, a Carmelite community with retreat centers in Colorado and Ireland. She studied languages for a career in international relations at Trinity College in Washington, D.C., before entering a monastery in 1967. Tessa is actively involved in Buddhist-Christian dialogues and international initiatives exploring world peace and planetary survival. She is the author of *Teresa of Avila: Ecstasy and Common Sense; Holy Daring: An Outrageous Gift to Modern Spirituality from Saint Teresa, the Grand Wild Woman of Ávila;* and *Teresa of Ávila: Mystical Writings,* and she recently recorded *Wild at Heart* for Sounds True and *Teresa of Avila: The Book of My Life* for Shambhala. She now lives alone in a log cabin in Crestone, Colorado, and is the cofounder of The Desert Foundation (www.desertfound.org), a circle of friends who explore the wisdom of the world's deserts, with a special emphasis on reconciliation between the three Abrahamic traditions that grow out of the desert, Judaism, Christianity, and Islam.

Dr. Ira Byock became involved in hospice and palliative care in 1978, during his family practice residency. At that time he helped found a hospice home care program for the indigent population served by the university hospital and county clinics of Fresno, California. Ira is a past president (1997) of the American Academy of Hospice and Palliative Medicine. He was a founder and principal investigator for the Missoula Demonstration Project, a community-based organization in Montana dedicated to the research and transformation of end-of-life experience locally, as a demonstration of what is possible nationally. From 1996 to 2006, he served as director of Promoting Excellence in End-of-Life Care, a national program of the Robert Wood Johnson Foundation.

Ira is currently director of Palliative Medicine at Dartmouth-Hitchcock Medical Center in Lebanon, New Hampshire. He is a professor at Dartmouth Medical School in the departments of Anesthesiology and Community & Family Medicine.

Ira's first book, *Dying Well* (1997), has become a standard in the field. His most recent book, *The Four Things That Matter Most* (Free Press, 2004), is a tool for helping people mend, tend, and nurture their most important relationships.

Ira has long been a public advocate for the rights of dying people and their families. He has authored numerous journal articles on the ethics and practice of hospice, palliative, and end-of-life care. Many of these are available at the DyingWell.org Web site (www.dyingwell.org). His essays have appeared in the *Washington Post* and *The Wall Street Journal*.

Joan Halifax Roshi is the head teacher and founder of Upaya Zen Center, a Zen Buddhist center in Santa Fe, New Mexico. A Ph.D., anthropologist, Buddhist teacher, and writer, Halifax has worked with dying people since 1970. She has been on the faculties of Columbia University, the University of Miami School of Medicine, the New School for Social Research, the Naropa Institute, and the California Institute for Integral Studies. Her books include *The Human Encounter with Death* (with Stanislav Grof); *Shamanic Voices; Shaman: The Wounded Healer; The Fruitful Darkness: A Journey Through Buddhist Practice and Tribal Wisdom;* and *Being with Dying: Cultivating Compassion and Fearlessness in the Presence of Death.* She founded The Ojai Foundation (an educational center), in 1979, and Upaya Zen Center (a Buddhist study center) in 1990. In 1994, she created the Project on Being with Dying as a way to train health-care professionals in contemplative care of the dying.

Netanel Miles-Yepez was born in Battle Creek, Michigan, in 1972, and is descended from a Sefardi family of crypto-Jews (*anusim,* "forced" converts) tracing their ancestry from Mexico all the way back to medieval Portugal and Spain. He studied History of Religions at Michigan State University and contemplative religion at Naropa University, specializing in nondual philosophies and comparative religion.

Unsatisfied with academics alone, Netanel moved to Boulder, Colorado, to become reacquainted with his family's lost tradition of Judaism and to study Hasidism and Sufism under Rabbi Zalman Schachter-Shalomi's personal guidance. Today, he is a *murshid* ("guide") and cofounder of the Desert Fellowship of the Message: The Inayati-Maimuni Tariqat of Sufi-Hasidim with

Reb Zalman, fusing the Sufi and Hasidic principles of spirituality espoused by Rabbi Avraham Maimuni in thirteenth-century Egypt with the teachings of the Ba'al Shem Tov and Hazrat Inayat Khan.

Netanel is currently the executive director of the Reb Zalman Legacy Project (www.rzlp.org), executive editor of *Spectrum: A Journal of Renewal Spirituality,* an advisor and editor for the Spiritual Paths Foundation and the Spiritual Paths Institute, and the author and editor of *Wrapped in a Holy Flame: Teachings and Tales of the Hasidic Masters* (Jossey-Bass, 2003); *The Common Heart: An Experience of Interreligious Dialogue* (Lantern Books, 2006); and *A Heart Afire: Stories and Teachings of the Early Hasidic Masters* (Jewish Publication Society, 2009).

He lives with his wife, Jennifer, in Boulder, Colorado.

Rabbi Zalman Schachter-Shalomi, better known as Reb Zalman, was born in Zholkiew, Poland, in 1924. Raised largely in Vienna, his family fled the Nazi oppression in 1938 and finally landed in New York City in 1941, settling in Brooklyn, where he enrolled in the yeshiva of the Lubavitcher Hasidim. He was ordained by Lubavitch in 1947. He received his master of arts degree in the Psychology of Religion in 1956 from Boston University and a Doctor of Hebrew Letters degree from Hebrew Union College in 1968.

He taught at the University of Manitoba, Canada, from 1956 to 1975 and was professor of Jewish Mysticism and Psychology of Religion at Temple University until his early retirement in 1987, when he was named professor emeritus. In 1995, he accepted the World Wisdom Chair at Naropa University in Boulder, Colorado, and officially retired from that post in 2004.

Throughout his long career, Reb Zalman has been an unending resource for the world religious community. He is the father of the Jewish Renewal and Spiritual Eldering movements, an active teacher of Hasidism and Jewish mysticism, and a participant in ecumenical dialogues throughout the world, including the widely influential dialogue with the Dalai Lama, documented in the book, *The Jew in the Lotus*. One of the world's foremost authorities on Jewish mysticism, he is the author of *Jewish with Feeling: A Guide to Meaningful Jewish Practice* (Riverhead Books, 2005) and *A Heart Afire: Stories and Teachings of the Early Hasidic Masters* (Jewish Publication Society, 2009). Reb Zalman currently lives in Boulder, Colorado, and continues to be active in mentoring his many students the world over. For more information, visit www.rzlp.org.

Marilyn Schlitz, Ph.D., is vice president of research at the Institute of Noetic Sciences and senior scientist at the Geraldine Brush Cancer Research Institute at the California Pacific Medical Center. Trained in medical anthropology and psi research, Marilyn has published numerous articles on cross-cultural healing, consciousness studies, distant healing, and the discourse of controversial science.

Marilyn has conducted research at Stanford University, Science Applications International Corporation, the Institute for Parapsychology, and the Mind Science Foundation; she has taught at Trinity, Stanford, and Harvard universities, and has lectured widely, including talks at the United Nations and the Smithsonian Institution. She serves on the Editorial Board of *Alternative Therapies,* is the leader of Esalen's Center for Theory and Research Working Group on Distant Healing Intentionality, and is on the Scientific Program Committee for the Consciousness Center at the University of Arizona, Tucson.

Mirabai Starr is an adjunct professor of philosophy and religious studies at the University of New Mexico and a certified grief counselor. She has studied a wide variety of religious traditions, including Hinduism, Judaism, Buddhism, Sufism, and Christianity, and is a critically acclaimed translator of the Spanish mystics, St. John of the Cross and St. Teresa of Avila. Her translations include *The Dark Night of the Soul* by St. John of the Cross, and *Interior Castle* and *The Book of My Life* by St. Teresa of Avila. She is also the editor of a series of devotional books from Sounds True: *St. Teresa of Avila, Saint Francis of Assisi, Saint Michael the Archangel, Saint John of the Cross, Our Lady of Guadalupe,* and *Hildegard of Bingen.*

The Spiritual Paths
Foundation

At the dawn of this new millenium, the possibilities have never been better for us to broaden and deepen our spiritual knowledge and to actualize our own spiritual potential. Cultural diversity, the Internet, advances in personal mobility, and the proliferation of new media have opened up seemingly infinite opportunities for us to explore, as never before possible, the world's spiritual treasures.

The Spiritual Paths Foundation provides a unique and holistic approach to the entire genre of interreligious activity in our day. Going well beyond the spiritual rapprochement of many interfaith events, Spiritual Paths offers a broad-based continuum of experiential, topic-oriented seminars and a comprehensive educational follow-up for attendees with today's leading spiritual teachers.

The Foundation promotes peace, respect, and mutual understanding between peoples of diverse religious and spiritual traditions. We explore and celebrate the spiritual dimension in the human quest to integrate mind, body, and spirit. We support the emergence of "InterSpirituality" as a new paradigm for a new millennium.

The primary goal is to give both budding and experienced spiritual seekers direct access to these teachers and an authentic taste of the world's major wisdom traditions. This is accomplished through our seminars, held around the country on thirty-six possible topics, as seen through the lenses of the major wisdom traditions and exemplars. Seminars are supported by our multimedia Spiritual Paths Web site (www.spiritualpaths .net), which serves as the informational hub of our educational activities. There, one may register for online seminars and continuing education (CEU) certificate programs; find information on numerous spiritual paths and topics; find information and guidance on authentic spiritual communities and teachers in your area; and discover books and audiovisual materials developed from the Spiritual Paths seminars, including lectures, group discussions, and interviews. The Web site also contains information on the Spiritual Paths Institute Master's Degree and Certificate Program in InterSpiritual Studies.

The areas of concentration for Spiritual Paths' seminars and curricula include the paths of the Arts, the Body, Contemplation and Meditation, Devotion, Love, Healing, Intellect and Metaphysics, the Mystic, Nature, Prayer and Ritual, Relationships and Service, and Wisdom; the questions of Reality, Immortality, Happiness, God/Faith, Freedom, Existence, Ethics, the Universe, Truth, Transformation, the Supernatural, and Spiritual Beings; the traditions of Buddhism, Hinduism, Christianity, Islam, Judaism, Africa, America, Europe, East Asia, South Asia, the Middle East, and Oceania.

The Spiritual Paths endeavor is an evolving experiment, and its philosophy is one of spiritual transformation. It is in no way an attempt to promote or impose any rigid dogma. Spiritual Paths only wishes to provide both highly accessible and accurate information on the world's spiritual paths, in a marriage of the best traditions of religious and academic scholarship, of spirituality, and of science.

EDWARD W. BASTIAN, PRESIDENT

THE SPIRITUAL PATHS INSTITUTE

"Humanity stands at a crossroads between horror and hope. In choosing hope, we must seed a new consciousness, a radically fresh approach to life drawing its inspiration from perennial spiritual and moral insights, intuition, and experience. We call this new awareness Interspiritual, implying not the homogenization of religion, but the recovering of the shared mystic heart beating in the center of the world's deepest spiritual traditions."

WAYNE TEASDALE, *THE MYSTIC HEART*

The religious landscape of the world is changing. No longer solely dominated by separate and securely entrenched religious institutions, the religious lives of people, especially people in the United States, Canada, and other postindustrial nations, are increasingly defined by a sense of individual freedom, universality, and association with more than one religious or spiritual tradition.

By encouraging InterSpirituality we do not intend the blending of religions or the ending of religious diversity. On the contrary, by InterSpirituality we mean the increasing spiritual creativity emerging from the meeting of, and dialogue between, the world's major religious traditions. This meeting acknowledges differences between religions and affirms the greater unity they all share. This unity provides the common ground from which religious diversity flowers. People are discovering that their respect for and love of the religion of their birth need not preclude a similar respect for the full range of human spiritual creativity.

This discovery is fueling the growing interest in InterSpiritual study, practice, and lifestyle. We aim, therefore, to encourage "the recovery of the shared mystic heart beating in the center of the world's deepest spiritual traditions." InterSpirituality is a profound way of working toward the goal of global understanding, respect, and peace by elucidating the common themes, methodologies, meanings, and truths of the world's religions while respecting the unique gifts and particularities of each tradition.

As InterSpirituality grows and becomes the norm for greater numbers of people, the need arises for serious scholarship and practical guidance that explores the nature of this emerging reality and helps people navigate the waters of InterSpiritual awakening. We support students in the deepening of their spiritual paths without constricting their perspective to one particular theological mind-set.

To meet these needs, and to further define and shape the emerging field of InterSpirituality, the Spiritual Paths Institute Program offers a two-year Certificate and Advanced Degree in InterSpiritual Wisdom.

The Spiritual Paths Institute curriculum on InterSpiritual Wisdom was developed by an InterSpiritual team of exceptional teachers, each authenticated within their respective traditions.

The program is based on a rigorous academic inquiry into the teachings of the world's sacred traditions combined with personally guided spiritual practice.

The thirty-six-credit program entails four semesters, each beginning with a five-day residential intensive retreat followed by distance learning in a tutorial and small-group format. The four semester themes are Metaphysics, Tranformation, Applied Spirituality, and Global Vision-Personal Commitment. Students may enroll at the Certificate or Advanced Degree levels, or as Auditors. Spiritual Paths is authorized by the Colorado Commission on Higher Education to offer a master's degree to qualified students.

This program will help professionals to apply InterSpiritual knowledge, principles, and practices to a variety of fields, including education, health care, environment, social work, psychology, consciousness studies, physics, cosmology, chaplaincy, media, the arts, and InterSpiritual counseling, mentoring, and ministry.

For more information, visit www.spiritualpaths.net/institute. E-mail: info@spiritualpaths.net, or call 805-695-0104.

Pathfinders

Cancer patients must navigate the often challenging, confusing, and lonely path from diagnosis to treatment to resolution. The Pathfinders program is designed to address the mind, body, and spiritual needs of each individual patient. Patients are matched with a Pathfinder, a trained professional with an advanced degree in social work, family counseling, or therapy. These Pathfinders serve as advocates for patients within the Duke University Health System, providing unbiased guidance on complementary medicine, self-care, mind-body techniques, end-of-life planning, and spiritual connectivity. With the help of their Pathfinders, patients become knowledgeable about the available resources at Duke and in their home community, which are important to their recovery.

Pathfinders are integral members of the patient's cancer treatment team, joining with the oncologist, nurses, and others to ensure that every patient receives the highest-quality medical and nursing care, and that his or her emotional, family, and spiritual needs are met. At the conclusion of their cancer treatment, patients are informed and skilled to cope with future challenges. Their families are prepared to support their loved one's personal recovery. Both patient and family are ready for survivorship.

THE PATHFINDERS PROGRAM

Pathfinders use an integrative approach to ensure that all areas of a patient's care are explored. They work from the knowledge that healing occurs when the whole person is cared for, including the body, mind, and spirit. Each patient is given a notebook that shows how nutrition, exercise, stress management, and other integrative therapies are used in conjunction with medicines and treatments to provide the best possible personal recovery. The Pathfinder works with the patient to help create an individualized self-care plan, which is updated regularly.

Pathfinder services:
- Patient and family education
- Support groups for patients and caregivers
- Nutrition and exercise education
- Relaxation/stress-reduction skills training
- Spiritual counseling
- Life Review and end-of-life planning

Additional therapies provided by certified practitioners at Duke or in the home community:
- Acupuncture
- Massage Therapy
- Yoga and Pilates

- Reiki
- Healing Touch

Referrals for these additional therapies are made with the approval of the patient's oncologist. All non-Duke practitioners are carefully screened. Pathfinders work in conjunction with each patient's traditional course of treatment. When properly combined with standard cancer treatments such as radiation or chemotherapy, complementary therapies may enhance wellness and quality of life.

Program components for patients:

- Pathfinder-Patient Relationship: The Pathfinder and patient establish a mutually respectful relationship of trust, open communication, and rejuvenating dialogue. The Pathfinder uses a range of patient education methods to teach coping skills endorsed by cancer survivors.
- Support Groups: Groups create a sense of belonging and provide a setting in which to learn from survivors and improve an individualized plan of self-care.
- Self-Care: The patient restarts previous nutrition or exercise regimens that have been discontinued with the onset of cancer. They learn new ways of strengthening their body through fitness and healthy foods. They learn about and use complementary therapies recommended and approved by their oncologist to help counteract debilitating physical effects of their illness and treatment.

- Life Review: The Pathfinder works with the patient to help restore life meaning that has been eroded by the prospect of a potentially terminal illness and a life-altering treatment process. Together, they focus on living fully.

Program components for the patient's environment:

- Caregiver and Family Relationship: The patient works with the Pathfinder to develop a mutually respectful relationship with the persons closest to them, so that concerns can be translated into helpful actions that support their personal recovery.
- Treatment Team and Institution: The Pathfinder assists the medical and nursing providers and administrators and staff within Duke to establish goals to meet the patient and family's social and psychological needs.
- Volunteers: With the Pathfinder, trained volunteers—many of them cancer survivors—assist the patient in meeting basic needs, including transportation requirements, as well as provide emotional support.
- The Community: Home health providers, hospice workers, employers, and other interested individuals can work with the Pathfinder to learn how they can contribute to a patient's recovery. Pathfinders advise congregations, social groups, and cancer advocates how the community as a whole can support persons with cancer.

PALLIATIVE CARE AND HOSPICE CARE

Integrative care is also beneficial to the patient who faces a progressive, incurable illness. As medicine and nursing shift to comfort care rather than cure, the Pathfinder and the patient revise their self-care plan. During this time, patients feel cared for by family, friends, and their treatment team. They continue to see how they are meaningfully involved in their care and believe they can cope with what is before them. Patients maximize the quality of both their remaining life and death.

Phone: 970-925-1226 (National Office)
Web site: www.pathfindersforcancer.com

About Sounds True

Sounds True was founded in 1985 with a clear vision: to disseminate spiritual wisdom. Located in Boulder, Colorado, Sounds True publishes teaching programs that are designed to educate, uplift, and inspire. We work with many of the leading spiritual teachers, thinkers, healers, and visionary artists of our time.

To receive a free catalog of tools and teachings for personal and spiritual transformation, please visit www.soundstrue.com, call toll-free at 800-333-9185, or write to us at the address below.

SOUNDS TRUE
PO Box 8010 / Boulder, CO 80306